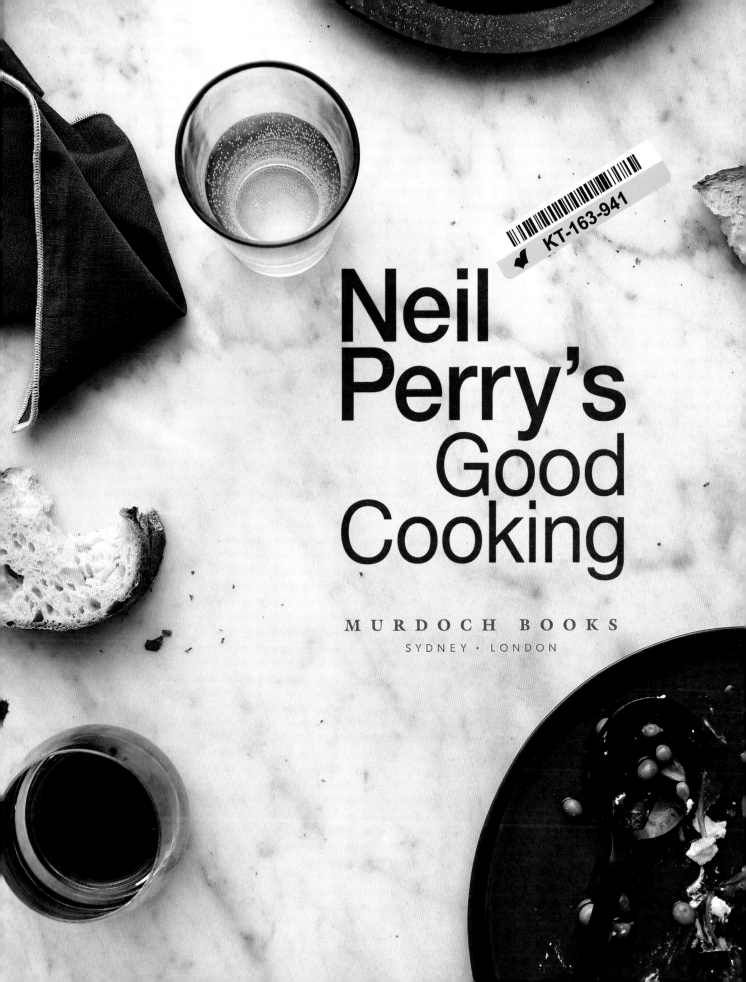

Neil Perry's Good Cooking

MURDOCH BOOKS

SYDNEY · LONDON

KT-163-941

To Margaret Perry
1927–2015

An amazing matriarch to a large family,
you are sorely missed. Rest in peace, my love. xx

Neil Perry AM is one of Australia's leading and most influential chefs. He has managed several award-winning restaurants in Australia and today concentrates on his flagship brand, the Rockpool Group, which includes Rockpool Bar & Grill, Sydney, Melbourne and Perth; Eleven Bridge, Sydney; Spice Temple, Sydney and Melbourne; Rosetta Ristorante, Melbourne; and various Burger Project venues across Australia. Neil has been creating menus for Qantas since 1997, continually redefining their dining and service, and is the author of *Rockpool*, *Simply Asian*, *Good Food*, *Balance & Harmony*, *Rockpool Bar & Grill*, *Easy Weekends*, *Simply Good Food*, *The Food I Love* and *Spice Temple*. He has also been a major television presenter for a number of series on the LifeStyle Channel.

If you own any of my cookbooks then you have my permission to glaze over now, as you are going to hear the same story again. I see no reason to change my modus operandi – it has, since the time I started cooking, been about one thing, and that is the quality of the produce, always driven by seasonality.

Good living is tied to good shopping and cooking. You don't need diets, you need a balanced diet. Eat plenty of fresh seasonal food, exercise by getting out in the world and, of course, drink responsibly – have a day or two off a week and don't drink to excess. (Health nuts might tell you not to drink wine at all, but then, how would life be worth living? I don't want to live to 100 and not enjoy myself.)

Try eating a good balance of dairy, nuts, vegetables, grains, poultry, meat and fish. Don't go for fad diets and I promise you will be able to maintain a healthy weight and not have to deprive yourself of anything. Just eat the naughty things in moderation.

My father taught me to live and eat with the seasons. I didn't realise it at the time, but boy was I lucky that he drummed it into me all those years ago: eating with him every day, helping in the garden and watching it grow, feeding the chooks and going on fishing trips with him. (Of course, the fact that he was a butcher, and a very good one, meant the meat we ate was always first class.) Eating food in season also gives you better value for money, as seasonal produce is generally cheaper.

I'm a truly multicultural cook, so here you'll find recipes from all around the globe – I love Korean, Japanese, Chinese, Mexican, Moroccan, Vietnamese and Thai food just as much as I love Italian, French, Spanish and whatever is Modern Australian food. Once you stock your pantry with the common ingredients that are used most in these cuisines, you'll be able to cook anything – have some fun with it.

Use the recipes as a guide, by all means – it's great to be inspired when cooking, not enslaved. Make sure you take note of the outcome and try to cook a little better each time. Cooking is a learned craft that you can improve if you wish.

I say this all the time: relax, and really *love* cooking for your family and friends. We have to eat to survive, so best to turn it into a joy, or life can be a real drag. Have fun and, most importantly, push yourself along at your own pace. There isn't a recipe in this book that can't be accomplished by someone who wants to put their mind to it.

Happy cooking – I believe through that, a happy and healthy life can be achieved.

Cheers,
Neil x

Kick off your day in style with one of the indulgent BREAKFASTS that start on PAGE 10, then discover my favourite selection of SMALL PLATES AND SOUPS from PAGE 18 – uncomplicated meals to enjoy as they are or share as part of a larger table. SALADS featuring the best seasonal produce follow on PAGE 70, then there's a clutch of comforting PASTA dishes beginning on PAGE 90. Plenty of ideas on how to cook delicious SEAFOOD start on PAGE 108, with POULTRY (PAGE 132), PORK AND VEAL (PAGE 158) and BEEF AND LAMB (PAGE 174) following. Far from merely side dishes, the VEGETABLE recipes from PAGE 198 can easily be the star of the show. Finally, round off an amazing meal with one of my easy DESSERTS, from PAGE 224.

I usually start the day with a simple breakfast of bircher muesli and fresh juice. However, on weekends, when I'm feeling a little decadent and need spoiling, I like something a bit more substantial. That's when these delicious dishes hit the spot.

Baked eggs with spicy sausage

Serves 4

A perfect dish for Sunday brunch; a truly delicious and decadent way to start the day. You can use ready-made harissa paste or you can make your own (see recipe on page 150), which gives a subtler flavour to the dish. Ready-made harissa can be seriously hot, so make sure you taste it before you add it.

1 teaspoon cumin seeds
$1/2$ teaspoon caraway seeds
1 spicy chorizo sausage
125 ml (4 fl oz/$1/2$ cup) extra virgin
   olive oil
1 red onion, sliced
3 garlic cloves, chopped
sea salt
2 red capsicums (peppers), diced
1 teaspoon thyme leaves, chopped
1 tablespoon flat-leaf (Italian) parsley
   leaves, chopped
1 teaspoon smoked paprika
harissa, to taste
2 tablespoons tomato paste
   (concentrated purée)
2 teaspoons red wine vinegar
2 teaspoons honey
2 x 400 g (14 oz) tins diced
   Italian tomatoes
8 free-range eggs
140 g (5 oz/$1/2$ cup) labna, at
   room temperature
1 small handful coriander (cilantro)
   leaves, chopped
crusty bread, to serve

Preheat the oven to 180°C (350°F).

Heat a large, wide, ovenproof frying pan over medium heat. Dry-fry the cumin and caraway seeds until fragrant. Remove and set aside.

Slice the chorizo lengthways into quarters, then cut into chunks. Add 2 tablespoons of the olive oil to the pan and fry the chorizo until golden. Remove and set aside with the spices.

Heat the remaining olive oil in the pan over low heat, then add the onion, garlic and sea salt and cook for 5 minutes. Increase the heat to medium and add the capsicums, thyme and parsley. Cook until the mixture is starting to get a good colour. Add the paprika, then return the chorizo and spices to the pan and stir for about 1 minute or until fragrant. Add the harissa and tomato paste and stir until the pastes are slightly coloured. Stir in the red wine vinegar, honey and tomatoes. Bring to a simmer and cook for 12–15 minutes. The sauce should have a great flavour and be slightly thickened but not too thick as you still need to cook the eggs in it. Add a little water if needed.

Take the pan off the heat and make eight wells in the sauce. Crack an egg into each well and use a fork to mingle the whites with the sauce without breaking the yolks. Transfer the pan to the oven and bake, checking regularly, for about 10–15 minutes or until the eggs are done to your liking.

As soon as the pan is out of the oven, dot spoonfuls of labna over the eggs and sauce, sprinkle with the chopped coriander and serve with lots of crusty bread.

Note
Use ready-made labna or make your own by spooning plain yoghurt into a strainer lined with muslin (cheesecloth) and suspending it over a bowl in the fridge for several hours or overnight, allowing the excess whey to drain away.

Turkish bread pockets

Makes 20

These savoury bread pastries are traditionally eaten in Turkey in the morning, often as a quick breakfast on the way to work, but they are just as good at lunchtime with a simple green salad. They are best eaten warm, straight from the oven. There are two different fillings – sprinkle the lamb-filled pastries with nigella seeds and the feta-filled pastries with sesame seeds so you can tell them apart when they're cooked.

1 tablespoon caster (superfine) sugar
1 tablespoon instant dried yeast
60 ml (2 fl oz/^{1}/$_4$ cup) milk, warmed
50 g (1^3/$_4$ oz) unsalted butter, melted
125 ml (4 fl oz/^{1}/$_2$ cup) olive oil
^{1}/$_2$ teaspoon sea salt
185 ml (6 fl oz/^{3}/$_4$ cup) sparkling
    mineral water, at room temperature
600 g (1 lb 5 oz/4 cups) plain
    (all-purpose) flour
1 free-range egg yolk, whisked with
    1 tablespoon water
2 teaspoons nigella seeds
2 teaspoons sesame seeds

Lamb filling
1 tablespoon extra virgin olive oil
1 brown onion, chopped
2 garlic cloves, chopped
1 teaspoon sea salt
250 g (9 oz) minced (ground) lamb
1 teaspoon ground coriander
1 teaspoon ground cumin
^{1}/$_4$ teaspoon chilli flakes
^{1}/$_4$ teaspoon ground cinnamon
2 tablespoons tomato paste
    (concentrated purée)
125 ml (4 fl oz/^{1}/$_2$ cup) tomato passata

Feta filling
200 g (7 oz/1^1/$_2$ cups) soft feta cheese
    in oil, well drained
5 g (^{1}/$_8$ oz/^{1}/$_4$ cup) flat-leaf (Italian) parsley
    leaves, chopped
2 tablespoons dill, chopped
1 teaspoon ground sumac
sea salt and freshly ground black pepper

Combine the sugar and yeast with the milk, butter and olive oil. Pour into the bowl of an electric mixer with a dough hook attachment. Add the salt and mineral water and begin mixing, then gradually add the flour. Knead well until you have a pliable, soft and non-sticky dough. (Alternatively, to make the dough by hand, sift the flour and salt into a large mixing bowl and make a well in the centre. Combine the sugar, yeast, milk, butter and olive oil, then pour into the well. Use a wooden spoon to start bringing the mixture together, gradually adding the mineral water as you go, then tip onto a lightly floured surface and knead until you have a pliable, soft and non-sticky dough.)

Cover the dough with a moist cloth and let it rest somewhere warm for 45 minutes or until doubled in size.

To make the lamb filling, heat the olive oil in a frying pan over medium heat. Add the onion, garlic and salt and sauté until softened. Add the lamb and spices and cook, stirring, to brown the meat, being careful not to burn the spices. Stir in the tomato paste and the passata. Bring to a simmer and stir over low heat for 5 minutes or until the mixture is flavoursome and reduced. Make sure it isn't too wet or the pastry will be soggy. Check the seasoning and allow to cool.

To make the feta filling, mix the feta, parsley, dill and sumac together, then taste and season with sea salt and black pepper if needed.

Divide the dough into 20 balls. Roll each ball into a disc about 2.5 mm (^{1}/$_{16}$ inch) thick. Divide the feta mixture among half the discs, then gather the dough up over the filling and pinch together to seal, making sure the filling is completely enclosed. Repeat with the lamb filling and remaining discs, then place on a lined baking tray, sealed side down. Set aside to rest somewhere warm for 15–20 minutes.

Meanwhile, preheat the oven to 180°C (350°F).

Brush the beaten egg yolk on the top of the pastries. Sprinkle the lamb-filled pastries with the nigella seeds and the feta-filled pastries with the sesame seeds. Bake for 20–30 minutes or until golden.

Note
Nigella seeds are popular in Turkish cooking and they give the pastries a distinct aroma and flavour. You can use poppy seeds if you prefer.

Huevos rancheros
Serves 4

I'm going to put it out there: this may not be the healthiest breakfast or brunch dish you've ever had, but it might well be the tastiest. Beans, tortillas and eggs are amazing together and I especially like them with lots of fresh coriander (cilantro) and hot sauce. You'll find most of the ingredients you need in a South American food store. Dry ricotta or another firm fresh cheese can be used as a substitute for the queso fresco.

vegetable oil, for frying
8 small corn tortillas
430 g (15$^1/_4$ oz) tinned refried beans
    (optional)
8 free-range eggs
120 g (4$^1/_4$ oz/1 cup) grated queso fresco
your choice of extra accompaniments,
    such as avocado, sour cream,
    coriander (cilantro) leaves, hot sauce
    or salsa verde

Tomato sauce
2 tablespoons vegetable oil
1 large brown onion, cut into 1.5 cm
    ($^5/_8$ inch) squares
1 red capsicum (pepper), cut into 1.5 cm
    ($^5/_8$ inch) squares
1 teaspoon dried oregano
1 teaspoon cumin seeds
1 x 400 g (14 oz) tin diced tomatoes
1 x 400 g (14 oz) tin red enchilada sauce
400 ml (14 fl oz) Fresh chicken stock
    (page 56)

Fresh tomato salsa
2 large tomatoes, finely diced
$^1/_2$ fresh jalapeño chilli, finely chopped,
    or to taste
$^1/_2$ small white onion, finely diced
1 large handful coriander (cilantro) leaves,
    finely chopped
lime juice, to taste
sea salt

To make the tomato sauce, heat the oil in a heavy-based saucepan over medium–high heat. Sauté the onion and capsicum until soft and lightly browned. Add the oregano and cumin and cook for about 1 minute. Add the tomatoes, enchilada sauce and stock, then increase the heat to high. Bring to the boil, stirring frequently, then reduce the heat to medium–low. Simmer for about 30 minutes or until the sauce has reduced and thickened.

To make the tomato salsa, combine all the ingredients in a bowl. Adjust the chilli, lime and salt to taste, then set aside.

Heat about 60 ml (2 fl oz/$^1/_4$ cup) vegetable oil in a small frying pan over medium heat. Test the oil with a small piece of tortilla to make sure it's ready – it should start to bubble immediately, but if it browns right away, it's too hot. Place a corn tortilla in the oil and cook for about 30 seconds, then flip over and cook for another 30 seconds. (You want the tortilla to be golden but not hard.) Drain on a plate lined with paper towel and keep warm while you cook the remaining tortillas.

Wipe out the small frying pan and heat the refried beans, if using.

Meanwhile, fry the eggs in batches in a large frying pan (I like to leave the yolks runny).

Put two corn tortillas on each serving plate and top with the refried beans and fried eggs. Spoon the tomato sauce over the top, sprinkle with the cheese and finish with the fresh salsa. Serve immediately with your choice of extra accompaniments.

Uncomplicated and unfussy … to feed a crowd or just for one … a tasty side or a small but perfectly formed meal … these delicious recipes will suit any occasion.

Thai-style fish cakes with cucumber relish

Serves 4 as a starter or as part of a shared banquet

By all means make your own curry paste as it's worth the effort, but by the same token, this recipe is easy to make with a good-quality ready-made curry paste. You can make the fish cakes a more substantial starter by putting some baby cos (romaine) leaves on the plates, adding the fish cakes and pouring the relish over the top as a dressing. Some ground roasted rice (see Note page 29) is a great textural addition on the top.

300 g ($10^1/_2$ oz) redfish or other inexpensive white-fleshed fish, roughly chopped
3 tablespoons Thai red curry paste
1 free-range egg
1 tablespoon fish sauce
1 teaspoon caster (superfine) sugar
5 kaffir lime leaves, finely shredded
2 snake (yard-long) beans, cut into thin rounds
vegetable oil, for deep-frying
lime wedges, to serve

Cucumber relish

60 ml (2 fl oz/$^1/_4$ cup) coconut vinegar
55 g (2 oz/$^1/_4$ cup) caster (superfine) sugar
sea salt
1 small cucumber
4 red Asian shallots, thinly sliced
1 cm ($^1/_2$ inch) piece fresh ginger, peeled and julienned
1 long fresh red chilli, seeded and julienned
1 small handful coriander (cilantro) leaves

To make the cucumber relish, combine the coconut vinegar, sugar, sea salt and 80 ml ($2^1/_2$ fl oz/$^1/_3$ cup) water in a small saucepan. Bring to the boil and stir until the sugar has dissolved. Remove from the heat, check the seasoning and set aside to cool completely.

Halve the cucumber lengthways and use a teaspoon to scrape out the seeds, then cut lengthways into thin slices. Stir the cucumber, shallots, ginger, chilli and coriander through the vinegar mixture and set aside.

Add the fish to a food processor with the curry paste, egg, fish sauce and sugar. Blend well, then transfer the mixture to a large bowl. Use your hands to scoop up the mixture and throw it back into the bowl several times until sticky; this is an important part of the process to give the fish cakes their texture. Incorporate the lime leaves and beans into the mixture. Mould the mixture into 5 cm (2 inch) discs.

Heat the vegetable oil in a wok over medium heat, ensuring the wok is stable, to 180°C (350°F) or until a small cube of bread browns in 15 seconds. Deep-fry the fish cakes in batches, turning once, for 4–5 minutes or until golden. Drain on paper towel and keep warm while you cook the remaining fish cakes.

Serve the fish cakes immediately with lime wedges and the cucumber relish on the side.

Note

Coconut vinegar is made from fermented coconut water and is normally found in health food stores. It is a low-acid vinegar that is cloudy and sweet compared to other vinegars. You could substitute it with rice vinegar or apple cider vinegar.

Roast globe artichokes with garlic and lemon mayonnaise

Serves 4 as a starter

Artichokes, boiled or grilled and served with mayonnaise or vinaigrette, are one of my favourite foods. Asparagus is great served this way as well. You could also roast the artichokes and just drizzle them with melted butter and lemon juice.

4 globe artichokes
1 lemon
80 ml (2 1/2 fl oz / 1/3 cup) extra virgin olive oil
8 unpeeled garlic cloves
sea salt and freshly ground black pepper
185 g (6 1/2 oz / 3/4 cup) whole-egg mayonnaise
1 tablespoon dijon mustard

Preheat the oven to 200°C (400°F).

Prepare the artichokes by cutting about 2.5 cm (1 inch) off the top with a sharp serrated knife. Clip the pointed tips off any remaining leaves using kitchen scissors. Cut off the artichoke stems to create a flat base so they sit easily on a plate. Gently scrape out the pinkish–purple leaves in the centre of each artichoke as well as the fuzzy 'choke' (these are inedible). Rinse the artichokes under running water. Finely grate the lemon zest and reserve it for the mayonnaise. Slice the lemon in half and rub it over all the cut areas of the artichokes to prevent discolouration. Reserve the lemon halves.

Take four large pieces of foil, drizzle a little of the olive oil in the centre of each and put an artichoke on top. Squeeze some lemon juice inside the cavity of each artichoke and add two garlic cloves. Season the artichokes well with sea salt and black pepper, then add a splash of olive oil on top. Wrap each artichoke in the foil, place on a baking tray and roast for 1 hour, depending on the size of the artichokes, until the centre is tender and the leaves pull away easily.

Unwrap the artichokes, remove one garlic clove from each artichoke and squeeze out the golden, soft and sweet garlic pulp from the skin into a mixing bowl. It should almost be the consistency of a purée, but you can use a fork to mash it until smooth if needed. Stir in the mayonnaise, mustard and reserved lemon zest, then season to taste. If you love garlic, add more garlic purée from the remaining garlic cloves.

Serve each of the artichokes with the garlic and lemon mayonnaise, a plate for the discarded tough leaves and a finger bowl for afterwards. You can scrape the tender flesh from the leaves with your teeth as you eat – that's part of the fun.

ROAST GLOBE ARTICHOKES WITH GARLIC AND LEMON MAYONNAISE

Adobo-marinated chicken tacos

Makes 16

Serve these with the Cabbage salad from page 47. A tomato salsa with roasted tomatoes mixed with chipotle chilli is also a great accompaniment. Look for dried chillies and corn tortillas in a South American food store or online. Any remaining Chilli purée can be refrigerated for another use.

1 kg (2 lb 4 oz) boneless, skinless
    free-range chicken thighs
2 tablespoons olive oil or vegetable oil
16 corn tortillas

Chilli purée
4 dried guajillo chillies, split and seeded
4 dried ancho chillies, split and seeded
1 small knob fresh ginger, peeled and
    finely chopped
1 teaspoon ground cumin
$1/2$ teaspoon freshly ground black pepper
$1^1/2$ teaspoons sea salt

To serve
sliced avocado
sliced white onion
finely chopped fresh 'angry' or hot chillies
coriander (cilantro) leaves (optional)
lime wedges

To make the chilli purée, combine the dried chillies in a large bowl and add enough hot water to cover them. Soak the chillies until they're soft, about 30 minutes. Drain and reserve the soaking water. Add the soaked chillies to a blender with the ginger, cumin, pepper, salt and 125 ml (4 fl oz/$1/2$ cup) of the soaking water and purée until very smooth. You'll probably need to poke and pulse the mixture to help it blend – don't be tempted to add more water because you want the purée to be as thick as possible.

Put the chicken thighs in a bowl, add 125 ml (4 fl oz/$1/2$ cup) of the chilli purée and rub it over the chicken until the meat is well coated. You can cook the chicken right away or, even better, marinate it for up to a few hours in the fridge.

Heat a large frying pan over medium–high heat. Add a thin layer of the olive or vegetable oil and cook the chicken in batches, turning once, until browned on both sides and just cooked through. It will take about 8–10 minutes per batch. Let the chicken rest for a few minutes, then slice it across the grain and dice or tear the meat.

While the chicken is resting, heat the tortillas on a hot dry grill or in a frying pan (don't use any oil) until steam rises – about 10 seconds on each side. As you heat them, pile the tortillas up and wrap in a clean tea towel or foil so they steam to soften and stay warm.

Fill the warm tortillas with the chicken, avocado, onion, fresh chillies and coriander, if using, and serve with the lime wedges alongside.

ADOBO-MARINATED CHICKEN TACOS

Scampi crudo with orange, pistachio and mint

Serves 8 as part of a shared starter

This Sicilian-inspired dish flies out the door at my Melbourne restaurant, Rosetta. The scampi are so sweet-tasting, with a very creamy texture. Raw prawns (shrimp) can be substituted if scampi are too hard to find. Raw tuna or kingfish also work well with this dressing.

1 orange
800 g (1 lb 12 oz) sashimi-quality scampi
sea salt and freshly ground black pepper
extra virgin olive oil, for drizzling
50 g (1 3/4 oz) unsalted pistachio nuts, roughly chopped
6 large mint leaves, finely shredded

Peel the orange with a small sharp knife, removing all of the white pith. Cut between the membranes to remove the segments.

Remove the tail meat from the scampi, discard the shells and devein. Cut in half lengthways and arrange on a platter.

Season the scampi well with sea salt and black pepper. Arrange on a platter and drizzle with olive oil, then add the orange segments. Scatter the pistachios and mint over the top and serve immediately.

SCAMPI CRUDO WITH ORANGE, PISTACHIO AND MINT

Warm skirt steak salad with tomatoes and chipotle dressing

Serves 4

Look for chipotle chillies in adobo sauce in a South American food store or online. The steak and chipotle dressing work equally well with refried beans in a tortilla, along with a salad of shredded cabbage, fresh tomato and chilli salsa.

80 ml (2^1/$_2$ fl oz/^{1}/$_3$ cup) extra virgin olive oil

400 g (14 oz) skirt (flank) steak

sea salt and freshly ground black pepper

2 garlic cloves, finely chopped

60 ml (2 fl oz/^{1}/$_4$ cup) beef stock or water

120 g (4^1/$_4$ oz) tinned chipotle chillies in adobo sauce

60 ml (2 fl oz/^{1}/$_4$ cup) lime juice

1 small frisée lettuce

45 g (1^1/$_2$ oz/1 cup) baby English spinach

2 tomatoes, chopped

4 baby radishes, thinly sliced

^{1}/$_2$ small red onion, cut into thin wedges

1 avocado, diced

1 handful coriander (cilantro) leaves

60 g (2^1/$_4$ oz) pecorino cheese

Warm 1 tablespoon of the olive oil in a heavy-based frying pan over medium–high heat. Season the steak with sea salt and black pepper and cook, turning only once, until both sides are well browned and cooked to your liking – about 4 minutes per side for medium–rare. Remove the steak from the pan and set aside to rest for about 3 minutes.

Reduce the heat under the same pan, then add the garlic and sauté for a few minutes. Pour in the stock or water, stir and deglaze the pan. Turn off the heat and add the chipotle chillies, lime juice and remaining olive oil. Season to taste.

Cut the steak across the grain into 5 mm (^{1}/$_4$ inch) strips, approximately 7–8 cm (2^3/$_4$–3^1/$_4$ inches) long.

Trim the frisée and cut the leaves into bite-sized pieces. Add to a bowl with the spinach, tomatoes, radishes, onion, avocado and coriander. Add the steak and the chipotle dressing (the greens will wilt slightly).

Divide the salad among four plates or large bowls, finely grate the cheese over the top and serve immediately.

WARM SKIRT STEAK SALAD WITH TOMATOES AND CHIPOTLE DRESSING

Mexican-style king prawn cocktail

Serves 4 as a starter

A great little Mexican feast. The chipotle chillies usually come in a large tin, so just transfer any leftovers to a container, cover with a little olive oil and keep them in the fridge. They're great chopped and added to butter to make an accompaniment for barbecued meat and seafood.

1 iceberg lettuce, finely shredded
1 corn cob, kernels cut off
1/2 red onion, thinly sliced
2 fresh jalapeño chillies, seeded and finely diced
1 avocado, finely diced
25 g (1 oz/1/2 cup) chopped coriander (cilantro)
extra virgin olive oil, for drizzling
juice of 2 limes
sea salt and freshly ground black pepper
16 large cooked king prawns (shrimp), peeled and deveined with tails intact

Sauce

60 ml (2 fl oz/1/4 cup) tomato sauce (ketchup)
5 drops Tabasco sauce
1 chilli from a tin of chipotle chillies in adobo sauce, minced
235 g (8 1/2 oz/1 cup) mayonnaise

To make the sauce, simply fold the tomato sauce, Tabasco and minced chipotle chilli through the mayonnaise until well incorporated.

Spread the shredded lettuce over a beautiful plate, then scatter the corn, red onion, jalapeño chillies, avocado and coriander over the top. Drizzle with the olive oil and lime juice and season with sea salt and black pepper.

Scatter the prawns over the salad and dollop a bit of sauce on each one to cover about half the prawn. Serve immediately.

Warm salad of spicy prawns

Serves 4 as a starter or as part of a shared banquet

Brilliant served with a steamed fish and some steamed rice, this spicy salad is also great made with minced (ground) chicken or pork. If you want it super spicy, roast a dried chilli until black, then grind it up and sprinkle it over the salad.

2 garlic cloves, chopped
2–4 fresh scud chillies, chopped
2 tablespoons peanut oil
250 g (9 oz) raw prawn (shrimp) meat, finely chopped
pinch of sea salt
1/2 small red onion, halved and thinly sliced
50 g (1 3/4 oz) green beans, thinly sliced
pinch of caster (superfine) sugar
1 tablespoon fish sauce
2 tablespoons lime juice
1 small handful mint leaves
1 small handful coriander (cilantro) leaves
1/2 baby cos (romaine) lettuce, leaves separated
1 teaspoon ground roasted rice (see Note)

Pound the garlic and chillies, to taste, in a mortar with a pestle to form a fine paste. Set aside.

Heat a wok over high heat until just smoking. Add the peanut oil and, when hot, stir-fry the prawn meat, sea salt, onion and beans for about 1 minute. Remove from the heat.

Add the garlic and chilli paste, sugar, fish sauce, lime juice, mint and coriander to the prawn mixture. Stir together and check the seasoning.

Arrange the lettuce leaves on a serving plate and spoon the prawn mixture on top. Sprinkle with the ground roasted rice and serve.

Note
To roast rice, dry-fry it in a frying pan over medium heat until it's just starting to colour, then tip it into a mortar and grind with a pestle.

Ceviche seafood salad with avocado, coriander and jalapeño

Serves 4 as a starter

Use any fish or shellfish in this fabulous seafood salad: crab, scallops, lobster or white-fleshed fish such as snapper would be great.

400 g (14 oz) sashimi-quality tuna
    and/or salmon
100 g (3 1/2 oz) sashimi-quality raw prawn
    (shrimp) meat
40 g (1 1/2 oz / 1/2 bunch) coriander (cilantro)
    leaves, stems and roots
250 ml (9 fl oz/1 cup) lime juice
2 garlic cloves, roughly chopped
1 fresh jalapeño chilli, seeded and
    roughly chopped
1 teaspoon sea salt
1 avocado, diced
1 large green butter lettuce,
    leaves separated
2 spring onions (scallions), thinly sliced
    on the diagonal
extra virgin olive oil, for drizzling

Cut the fish and prawns into 1–2 cm (1/2– 3/4 inch) chunks and place in a non-reactive bowl.

Pick and wash the coriander leaves, then set aside for garnishing. Using a paring knife, scrape the dirt away from the coriander roots, then wash the roots and stems. Chop and place in a blender with the lime juice, garlic, chilli and sea salt. Process until smooth.

Pour the coriander mixture over the seafood and leave to marinate. How long it 'cooks' is up to you – you can eat it right away, or leave it in the fridge for up to 2 hours.

Pour off half the marinating liquid and set aside. Toss the avocado with the seafood and check the seasoning.

Divide the lettuce among four serving plates and spoon the seafood mixture into the centre. Drizzle some of the reserved marinade over the salad and garnish with the spring onions and coriander leaves. Drizzle with extra virgin olive oil and serve immediately.

CEVICHE SEAFOOD SALAD WITH AVOCADO, CORIANDER AND JALAPEÑO

Pork and kimchi fritters with spring onion dipping sauce

Makes about 15

I'm a fan of anything with kimchi, and these fritters are no exception. They go really well with rice and you could serve them alongside other Korean-inspired dishes as part of a banquet. The Korean-flavoured seafood stew (page 108) and the Korean spice-rubbed chicken (page 146) would be great choices.

400 g (14 oz/2 cups) dried mung beans
50 g (1^3/$_4$ oz/^{1}/$_4$ cup) glutinous white rice
125 g (4^1/$_2$ oz/^{1}/$_2$ cup) kimchi, finely chopped, plus 125 ml (4 fl oz/^{1}/$_2$ cup) of the pickling liquid
1 teaspoon fish sauce
pinch of sea salt
125 ml (4 fl oz/^{1}/$_2$ cup) Korean soy sauce
60 ml (2 fl oz/^{1}/$_4$ cup) sesame oil
vegetable oil, for shallow frying
2 tablespoons rice vinegar
2 tablespoons gochugaru (Korean chilli powder)
3 spring onions (scallions), thinly sliced

Pork belly
300 g (10^1/$_2$ oz) pork belly
3 cm (1^1/$_4$ inch) knob fresh ginger, peeled and thinly sliced
2 spring onions (scallions), cut into 5 cm (2 inch) lengths
1 teaspoon sea salt

Combine the mung beans and rice in a bowl and rinse in a few changes of cold water. Cover with plenty of fresh water and leave to soak for at least 6 hours, preferably overnight.

For the pork belly, put the pork in a large saucepan, cover with water and bring to the boil. Drain and rinse the pork, wipe clean and return to the pan. Add the ginger, spring onions and sea salt, cover with water and bring to the boil. Reduce the heat to low, cover and gently simmer for 1^1/$_2$ hours or until the pork is tender. Drain the pork and leave to cool, then remove and discard the skin. Finely chop or shred the meat.

Drain the mung beans and rice well and transfer to a food processor. Add 125 ml (4 fl oz/^{1}/$_2$ cup) fresh water, the kimchi pickling liquid, fish sauce, sea salt and 1 teaspoon each of the soy sauce and sesame oil. Blend to a coarse purée (not too smooth). Transfer to a bowl and fold through the chopped kimchi and pork.

Heat the oil in a non-stick frying pan over medium heat. Spoon the batter into the pan, using about 60 ml (2 fl oz/^{1}/$_4$ cup) for each fritter. Cook for a couple of minutes until golden brown and crispy, then flip and cook the other side for another few minutes. Drain the fritters on paper towel and keep warm while you cook the remaining batter.

Quickly make the dipping sauce by combining the remaining soy sauce and sesame oil with the rice vinegar, gochugaru and spring onions. Serve the sauce alongside the hot crispy fritters.

Black pepper tofu with eggplant

Serves 4–6 as part of a shared banquet

Simply serve this with rice for an awesome meal. I've used the firm pressed tofu, but the sauce and eggplant are also great spooned over silken tofu that has been steamed until warm, or floured and fried so that it's crisp on the outside and meltingly soft inside.

2 teaspoons sichuan peppercorns
50 g (1 3/4 oz / 1/3 cup) plain (all-purpose) flour
pinch of sea salt
2 teaspoons black peppercorns
1 tablespoon peanut oil, plus extra for shallow frying
2 small Japanese eggplants (aubergines), thickly sliced
400 g (14 oz) firm tofu, cubed
1 small red onion, chopped
1 small red capsicum (pepper), chopped
1 long fresh red chilli, thinly sliced
2 garlic cloves, finely chopped
60 ml (2 fl oz / 1/4 cup) Fresh chicken stock (page 56)
2 teaspoons light soy sauce
1 tablespoon oyster sauce
1 teaspoon caster (superfine) sugar
2 spring onions (scallions), thinly sliced
1 small handful coriander (cilantro) leaves

Dry-fry the sichuan peppercorns in a wok over high heat for 20 seconds, then reduce the heat and stir for about 1 minute until their fragrance is released. Transfer the peppercorns to a mortar and crush with a pestle, then mix with the flour and sea salt. Crush the black peppercorns separately and set aside.

To shallow fry the eggplant slices, heat plenty of peanut oil in the wok over high heat, ensuring the wok is stable. When just smoking, add the eggplant slices and cook until golden brown on both sides, then drain on paper towel. Toss the tofu in the seasoned flour and shallow fry until golden all over with a thin crust. Transfer to a plate and wipe out the wok.

Add 1 tablespoon of the peanut oil to the wok. When just smoking, add the onion, capsicum, chilli, garlic and crushed black peppercorns and stir-fry until fragrant. Add the stock, soy sauce, oyster sauce and sugar and cook until slightly reduced. Check the seasoning, then add the tofu and eggplant to the sauce and toss to warm through.

Spoon the tofu mixture into a large serving bowl and serve garnished with the spring onions and coriander.

Seafood antipasto

Serves 4–8 as part of a shared banquet

A wonderful dish we serve at my Melbourne restaurant Rosetta; the lemon oil goes so well with the seafood. Please use any seafood you like – the dressing will be perfect with absolutely everything. Mussels are a great substitute for the clams or you could use a mixture of both. Just remember to clean the mussels and pull out the hairy beards.

600 g (1 lb 5 oz) clams (vongole)

330 g (11¹/2 oz) whole octopus with tentacles, gutted and cleaned, thawed if frozen

2 small squid with tentacles, about 330 g (11¹/2 oz), cleaned

450 g (1 lb) raw prawns (shrimp), shells on

80 ml (2¹/2 fl oz/¹/3 cup) white wine

30 ml (1 fl oz) lemon oil, or to taste

sea salt and freshly ground black pepper

2 celery stalks, leaves reserved, finely chopped

1 tablespoon finely chopped flat-leaf (Italian) parsley

2 garlic cloves, finely chopped

Soak the clams in cold water for 15 minutes, then drain and rinse well.

If you are using fresh octopus, beat it with a meat hammer to tenderise it (you don't need to do this if you are using frozen octopus, as freezing has a tenderising effect). Rinse well under cold running water, wiping with a clean sponge to remove any excess saltiness. Bring a large saucepan of water to the boil (do not add salt as this will toughen the octopus). Add the octopus, cover and reduce the heat to low. Gently simmer for 20–30 minutes or until tender. Drain well and cut the octopus into bite-sized pieces.

Meanwhile, bring another saucepan of water to the boil. Add the squid and simmer over low heat for 10 minutes, then remove with a slotted spoon. Allow to cool, then separate the tentacles from the squid and slice the squid bodies into strips.

Add the prawns to the pan of squid water and simmer for 2 minutes or until they have changed colour and are just cooked. Remove with a slotted spoon. Allow to cool, then peel and devein.

Place the clams and white wine in a large saucepan over high heat. Cover and cook, shaking the pan occasionally, until the clams have opened. Remove from the heat and strain, reserving the cooking liquid and discarding any clams that haven't opened.

Whisk 50 ml (1¹/2 fl oz) of the strained clam cooking liquid with the lemon oil, sea salt and black pepper to taste.

Put the octopus, squid, prawns, clams, chopped celery and celery leaves in a shallow serving dish. Drizzle the dressing over the seafood. Scatter with the parsley and garlic and serve immediately.

Note

If the clams are packaged and prewashed there is no need to soak them – just remove them from the packet and rinse.

SEAFOOD ANTIPASTO

White peach cocktails with lobster sandwiches

Serves 2 as a small starter

A bit of luxury, but if you want to dial it down a bit, cooked king prawns (shrimp) or crab meat are awesome too. For that matter, shredded roast chicken stirred through the mayo is also pretty darn good.

White peach cocktails
1 white peach, peeled and diced
300 ml (10^1/$_2$ fl oz) prosecco

Lobster sandwiches
120 g (4^1/$_4$ oz/^{1}/$_2$ cup) whole-egg mayonnaise
grated zest and juice of ^{1}/$_2$ lemon
2 teaspoons dill, chopped
1 tablespoon chopped chives
sea salt and freshly ground black pepper
350 g (12 oz) cooked lobster tail meat, chopped
butter, softened
6 slices very fresh white bread

To make the cocktails, gently crush the peach in a mortar with a pestle until it becomes a purée. Place in the fridge to chill along with two champagne glasses.

To make the sandwiches, combine the mayonnaise, lemon zest, lemon juice, herbs, sea salt and black pepper in a bowl. Mix well and check the seasoning. Mix the lobster meat through the mayonnaise.

Butter the bread and then use the filling to make three sandwiches. Press the outside edges of the sandwiches together to seal, then trim away the crusts and cut each sandwich in half.

Add the peach purée and prosecco to a metal cocktail shaker. Stir to combine, but do not shake. Pour into the chilled champagne glasses and serve immediately with the lobster sandwiches.

Chilled cucumber and ginger soup

Serves 4 as a small starter

The best no-fuss soup recipe ever, and incredibly delicious. It's the ideal start to a midsummer feast. You can change the flavour profile enormously simply by changing the herb you use. Try swapping the dill with coriander (cilantro) and the crème fraîche with yoghurt.

10 small Lebanese (short) cucumbers
2 teaspoons finely grated fresh ginger
chardonnay vinegar, to taste
sea salt and freshly ground white pepper
2 tablespoons crème fraîche
2 tablespoons dill, chopped

Peel and dice the cucumbers. Add to a food processor with the ginger and blend until the mixture forms a thick, smooth purée. Push the purée through a fine sieve and chill.

Just before serving, season the soup with chardonnay vinegar, sea salt and white pepper to taste.

Divide the chilled soup among four small bowls or cups. Add a small dollop of crème fraîche to each one and sprinkle with the dill to serve.

Quick Vietnamese chicken and prawn coleslaw

Serves 4

Ideal for lunch alongside some steamed rice; you could poach a chicken yourself, but I like the fact that some of the work is already done for you. A lovely white flaky fish would also work well in place of the chicken or, to make this a cracking vegetarian salad, replace the meat and seafood with some daikon radish, Chinese celery and cucumber and use tamari instead of fish sauce for the dressing.

1 small roasted or barbecued free-range chicken, organic if possible
6 cooked large king prawns (shrimp), peeled and deveined
1 carrot, julienned
200 g (7 oz/2 2/3 cups) shredded cabbage
1 small red onion, cut into thin rings
40 g (1 1/2 oz/2 cups) fragrant mixed herbs, such as Vietnamese mint, mint and coriander (cilantro)
1 1/2 tablespoons crispy fried shallots, plus 2 teaspoons to serve
1 1/2 tablespoons crushed roasted unsalted peanuts, plus 2 teaspoons to serve

Nuoc cham dressing
2 long fresh red chillies, finely chopped
1 garlic clove, finely chopped
1 tablespoon caster (superfine) sugar
60 ml (2 fl oz/1/4 cup) fish sauce
2 tablespoons rice vinegar
2 tablespoons lime juice

To make the dressing, pound the chillies, garlic and sugar in a mortar with a pestle. Add the fish sauce, rice vinegar and 60 ml (2 fl oz/1/4 cup) water and stir to dissolve the sugar. Set aside for about 15 minutes for the flavours to mingle. Stir in the lime juice and taste to check the balance of flavours.

Pull the chicken meat off the bones, tear it into bite-sized pieces and add it to a large bowl. Cut the prawns in half lengthways and add them to the bowl.

Add the carrot, cabbage, onion, herbs, fried shallots and peanuts to the bowl. Pour the dressing over the salad, mix well and transfer to a large serving bowl. Serve immediately, garnished with the extra fried shallots and peanuts.

QUICK VIETNAMESE CHICKEN AND PRAWN COLESLAW

Sticky pork skewers with spicy lime dipping sauce

Serves 4

For the best flavour, cook the skewers over a charcoal grill to impart a smoky flavour. Serve them with some soft-boiled eggs, steamed rice and salad for a simple but flavoursome meal.

600 g (1 lb 5 oz) pork neck or shoulder, cut into 2 cm (3/4 inch) pieces
80 ml (2 1/2 fl oz / 1/3 cup) coconut cream

Marinade

1/2 teaspoon white peppercorns
2 garlic cloves, chopped
2 tablespoons finely chopped coriander (cilantro) roots and stems
pinch of sea salt
2 tablespoons finely grated palm sugar (jaggery)
1 tablespoon fish sauce
1 tablespoon soy sauce
2 teaspoons oyster sauce

Dipping sauce

1 1/2 tablespoons thinly sliced spring onions (scallions)
1 1/2 tablespoons finely chopped coriander (cilantro) leaves
2 tablespoons fish sauce, or to taste
juice of 1 lime, or to taste
1 teaspoon grated palm sugar (jaggery), or to taste
2 teaspoons ground roasted rice (see Note page 29)
2 teaspoons chilli flakes

Make the marinade by pounding the peppercorns in a mortar with a pestle until roughly ground. Add the garlic, coriander and sea salt and pound into a fine paste. Stir through the palm sugar, fish sauce, soy sauce and oyster sauce.

Combine the pork pieces with the marinade and refrigerate for at least 3 hours or overnight.

Soak 12 wooden skewers in water for several hours or overnight.

To make the dipping sauce, mix all the ingredients in a bowl. Taste and add more fish sauce, lime juice or palm sugar if necessary. The sauce should be a balance of hot, sour, salty and sweet.

Preheat a gas or coal barbecue on medium heat.

Thread the marinated pork pieces close together onto the skewers to prevent them from drying out while cooking. Barbecue the skewers, brushing occasionally with the coconut cream and turning often, until the pork is caramelised and just cooked through.

Serve the pork skewers with the dipping sauce alongside.

Note
Always soak wooden skewers long enough so they don't burn when grilling – overnight is a good idea or at least a few hours.

STICKY PORK SKEWERS WITH SPICY LIME DIPPING SAUCE

Spicy barbecued chicken wings

Serves 4–8 as part of a shared banquet

To make a great shared meal, you only need add rice and some steamed greens to this. The chicken wings don't take long to cook on the barbecue as they are essentially ready to go once they have been blanched. You won't believe how tender twice-cooking makes them.

16 chicken wings
mint leaves, coriander (cilantro) leaves
    and lemon wedges, to serve

Marinade
4 garlic cloves, chopped
3 cm (1¼ inch) piece fresh ginger,
    peeled and minced
1 teaspoon ground coriander
½ teaspoon ground cinnamon
1 teaspoon smoked paprika
1 teaspoon chilli flakes
115 g (4 oz/⅓ cup) honey
60 ml (2 fl oz/¼ cup) soy sauce
80 ml (2½ fl oz/⅓ cup) peanut oil
juice of 1 lemon
sea salt

Bring a large saucepan of salted water to the boil, add the chicken wings and gently simmer for 10 minutes. Remove the pan from the heat and allow the chicken wings to cool in the water for 1 hour. Drain and pat dry.

Mix all the marinade ingredients together in a large bowl. Toss the chicken wings through the mixture and leave to marinate for 1 hour.

Preheat a barbecue on high heat.

Remove the chicken wings from the marinade and place in a bowl. Pour the marinade into a large saucepan and bring to the boil, then reduce the heat and simmer for 5 minutes or until reduced to a nice saucy consistency.

Meanwhile, cook the chicken wings on the hot barbecue for 2 minutes on each side or until they caramelise and char. Brush the charred wings with the reduced marinade.

Pile the chicken wings onto a large serving platter and sprinkle with the mint and coriander leaves. Serve immediately with lemon wedges.

Note
Refrigerate the chicken wings if you are marinating them for more than 1 hour. Take them out of the fridge 30 minutes before cooking.

SPICY BARBEC'JED CHICKEN WINGS

Cauliflower fritters with tomato chilli relish

Serves 4

Use any vegetable that grates well to make these fritters. Store any left-over relish in the fridge and use it anywhere you would normally use tomato sauce – it will last for a few weeks.

2 tablespoons grapeseed oil
1 large red onion, roughly chopped
1 cauliflower, about 900 g (2 lb),
    coarsely grated
3 large free-range eggs
100 g (3 1/2 oz / 2/3 cup) plain
    (all-purpose) flour
pinch of freshly ground white pepper
1 handful mint leaves, chopped
1 handful dill sprigs, chopped
200 g (7 oz) sheep's milk feta cheese,
    crumbled
sea salt
olive oil, for shallow frying

Tomato chilli relish
2 tablespoons grapeseed oil
1/2 small brown onion, finely chopped
1 garlic clove, finely chopped
1/2 small red capsicum (pepper),
    finely chopped
1 long fresh red chilli, seeded and
    finely chopped
1 teaspoon finely grated fresh ginger
400 g (14 oz) roma (plum) tomatoes, diced
100 ml (3 1/2 fl oz) cider vinegar
45 g (1 1/2 oz) caster (superfine) sugar
35 g (1 1/4 oz) light brown sugar
juice of 1/2 lemon
1/2 teaspoon sea salt
1 clove
1/2 cinnamon stick

To make the relish, heat the grapeseed oil in a heavy-based saucepan over low heat. Sauté the onion, garlic, capsicum, chilli and ginger for 10 minutes or until the vegetables are soft. Stir in the remaining ingredients and gently simmer for about 1 hour or until the mixture has thickened. Taste and adjust the seasoning.

For the fritters, heat the grapeseed oil in a large frying pan over medium heat and sauté the red onion until soft and slightly coloured. Add the cauliflower and sauté for another few minutes. Transfer the mixture to a colander to cool slightly and allow any excess liquid to drain away.

Whisk the eggs with the flour and white pepper in a large bowl until well blended, then stir through the herbs, feta and cauliflower mixture. Season to taste with sea salt. If the mixture is too runny, add a little more flour. Form the mixture into fritters 40–50 g (1 1/2–1 3/4 oz) each and place on a tray, ready for frying.

Heat the olive oil in a large frying pan over medium–low heat. Cook the fritters in batches until they are golden on both sides and just cooked through. Drain on paper towel.

Serve the warm fritters with a dollop of the tomato chilli relish.

Duck carnitas tacos

Makes 12

The term 'carnitas' normally applies to pork that has been poached and then fried to make it both tender and crispy. I have applied the same method to duck and the result is awesome. I like to serve these with a cabbage salad – it adds a great texture and is very refreshing.

6 duck legs
2 small white onions, sliced
1 garlic bulb, cut in half
1 cinnamon stick, broken into pieces
1 teaspoon ground cumin
1 tablespoon sea salt, plus extra to taste
1 orange, quartered
freshly ground black pepper
2 limes, quartered
12 flour tortillas

Tomatillo chipotle salsa

400 g (14 oz) tinned tomatillos, rinsed
    and drained
3 garlic cloves
2 chillies from a tin of chipotle chillies
    in adobo sauce, including a little
    of the sauce
sea salt
juice of 2 limes

Cabbage salad

1/4 cabbage, shredded
1 white onion, thinly sliced
80 g (2 3/4 oz/1 bunch) coriander
    (cilantro), chopped

Preheat the oven to 160°C (315°F).

Place the duck legs, onions, garlic, cinnamon, cumin and sea salt in a casserole dish. Squeeze the orange juice over the top, add the orange skins and mix everything together well. Cover and slide into the oven. Cook for about 2 hours or until the meat comes easily off the bone.

While the duck is cooking, make the salsa. Add the tomatillos, garlic and 60 ml (2 fl oz/1/4 cup) water to a small saucepan and cook, stirring from time to time, for about 10 minutes, then add the chillies and a little of the adobo sauce. Cool slightly, then use a blender or food processor to purée the sauce until very smooth. Season to taste with sea salt and lime juice, then set aside.

To make the salad, combine the cabbage and onion in a salad bowl and sprinkle with the coriander. Set aside.

Remove the duck legs from the casserole. Strain the liquid and fat through a sieve into a bowl. Place this in the fridge so the liquid and fat separate and the fat starts to solidify.

When the duck legs are cool enough to handle, pull the meat off the bones in large chunks. Carefully scoop out 2 tablespoons of the duck fat and heat in a large frying pan over medium–high heat. Add the duck meat and cook, stirring occasionally, for about 8 minutes or until golden brown and crisp. Season to taste with sea salt and black pepper, then arrange on a platter, surrounded by the lime quarters.

Heat the tortillas on a hot dry grill or in a frying pan (don't use any oil) until steam rises – about 10 seconds on each side. As you heat them, pile the tortillas up and wrap in a clean tea towel or foil so they steam to soften and stay warm.

To serve, put the tortillas, duck, cabbage salad and salsa on the table. Assemble the tacos by adding the duck, salad, salsa and a little squeeze of lime to the tortillas.

Barbecued baby pork back ribs with smoky barbecue sauce

Serves 4

Pre-cooking the ribs makes them super-tender and if you finish cooking them on the barbecue over charcoal and wood, you will have the best-ever smoky ribs.

2 racks baby pork back ribs, about
   1 kg (2 lb 4 oz) each
lime wedges, to serve

Spice rub
2 garlic cloves
2 teaspoons sea salt
2 teaspoons light brown sugar
$1/2$ teaspoon dried oregano
$1/4$ teaspoon ground cumin
2 teaspoons ground coriander
2 teaspoons smoked paprika
2 teaspoons freshly ground black pepper
1 tablespoon ancho chilli powder

Smoky barbecue sauce
1 tablespoon vegetable oil
1 red onion, chopped
2 garlic cloves, chopped
pinch of sea salt
4 chillies from a tin of chipotle chillies
   in adobo sauce
1 x 400 g (14 oz) tin diced tomatoes
125 ml (4 fl oz/$1/2$ cup) apple cider vinegar
80 ml (2$1/2$ fl oz/$1/3$ cup) dark soy sauce
150 g (5$1/2$ oz) light brown sugar

To make the spice rub, pound the garlic with the sea salt in a mortar with a pestle, then mix in the remaining ingredients.

Rub the spice mixture evenly into the ribs on both sides and leave to marinate while you prepare the sauce.

Preheat the oven to 150°C (300°F).

To make the sauce, heat the vegetable oil in a saucepan over medium heat. Sauté the onion with the garlic and salt until starting to turn golden. Stir in the remaining ingredients and bring to a simmer. Cook for about 5 minutes to reduce the sauce, then process with a stick blender until smooth.

Baste the ribs with the sauce, wrap completely in foil and place on a baking tray. Bake for about 1$1/2$ hours or until the meat is tender when tested with a fork.

Put the remaining sauce in a small saucepan and cook on the stovetop until it reduces to a sticky glaze.

Preheat a barbecue on medium heat. Remove the ribs from the foil and cook, turning and basting them occasionally with the glaze, for 8–10 minutes or until charred and sticky.

Slice the ribs and serve stacked on a platter with the lime wedges.

Note
Ancho chilli is a milder style of chilli used in Mexican cooking. Look for the ancho chilli powder and chipotle chillies in adobo sauce in a South American food store or online.

BARBECUED BABY PORK BACK RIBS WITH SMOKY BARBECUE SAUCE

Sweet potato, chilli and lime soup with tortilla crisps

Serves 4–6

The sweet potato could be substituted with pumpkin (squash) for an equally great result, and this soup would also be good made with corn. I reckon you could use frozen corn kernels and it would be very easy and tasty.

1 tablespoon vegetable oil, plus extra for deep-frying
3 dried ancho chillies, soaked and chopped
1 brown onion, diced
1 garlic clove, finely chopped
2 teaspoons sea salt
freshly ground black pepper
500 g (1 lb 2 oz) peeled orange sweet potatoes, cut into 2 cm (3/4 inch) pieces
1 litre (35 fl oz/4 cups) Fresh chicken stock (page 56), plus extra if needed
100 g (3 1/2 oz) corn tortillas
1 tablespoon lime juice
sour cream, to serve
coriander (cilantro) leaves, to serve

Heat the 1 tablespoon oil in a large saucepan over low heat. Add the chopped chillies, onion, garlic, sea salt and black pepper and cook for about 10 minutes or until the onion is soft. Add the sweet potatoes and stock, bring to a simmer and cook for about 20 minutes or until the sweet potatoes are soft. Allow the soup to cool slightly, then blend or process until smooth. You can add a little extra stock or water to thin it if you like.

While the soup is cooling, cut the tortillas into strips. Heat the oil in a large heavy-based saucepan or deep-fryer to about 180°C (350°F) or until a small cube of bread browns in 15 seconds. Deep-fry the tortilla strips in batches until golden and crisp. Drain on paper towel.

Stir the lime juice into the soup and check the seasoning. Serve the soup in deep bowls topped with a spoonful of sour cream, some tortilla crisps, coriander leaves and black pepper.

Note

Look for dried ancho chillies in a South American food store or online.

SWEET POTATO, CHILLI AND LIME SOUP WITH TORTILLA CRISPS

Carrot and cumin soup with coriander yoghurt

Serves 4

This soup has flown on Qantas often, as it's always been so popular. Along with a zucchini (courgette) soup we do, it's by far the most requested by passengers – they all want the recipe.

8 carrots, peeled and quartered
  lengthways
1 teaspoon cumin seeds
80 ml (2 $^1/_2$ fl oz / $^1/_3$ cup) extra virgin
  olive oil
25 g (1 oz) butter
2 brown onions, roughly chopped
2 garlic cloves, finely chopped
1 small knob fresh ginger, peeled
  and finely grated
sea salt
pinch of sugar
1 large all-purpose potato (e.g. sebago),
  peeled and chopped
1.25 litres (44 fl oz / 5 cups) Fresh chicken
  stock (page 56), plus extra if needed
80 ml (2 $^1/_2$ fl oz / $^1/_3$ cup) thin
  (pouring) cream
freshly ground black pepper

Coriander yoghurt
260 g (9 $^1/_4$ oz / 1 cup) Greek-style yoghurt
1 small handful coriander (cilantro) leaves,
  finely chopped
1 sprig mint leaves, finely chopped
$^1/_2$ garlic clove, finely chopped
squeeze of lemon juice
sea salt and freshly ground white pepper

Preheat the oven to 160°C (315°F). Toss the carrots with half the cumin seeds and half the olive oil in a large roasting tin. Roast, shaking the pan occasionally, for about 1 hour or until the carrots are tender and lightly browned.

Meanwhile, dry-fry the remaining cumin seeds in a small frying pan over low heat until fragrant. Crush the toasted seeds in a mortar with a pestle until finely ground.

Heat the remaining olive oil and the butter in a large heavy-based saucepan. Add the onions, garlic, ginger, sea salt and ground cumin seeds. Sweat over very low heat for about 10 minutes or until the onion is very soft. Add the sugar and potato and cook, stirring, for a further 5 minutes.

Add the roasted carrots and stock to the pan and simmer, covered, for about 30 minutes or until the vegetables are very tender. Process with a stick blender until very smooth. Stir in the cream and pepper. Add more stock if necessary to give the desired consistency.

Meanwhile, to make the coriander yoghurt, simply mix everything together and season to taste.

Divide the soup among four large bowls, add a dollop of the coriander yoghurt and serve sprinkled with black pepper.

CARROT AND CUMIN SOUP WITH CORIANDER YOGHURT

Prawn and ginger congee

Serves 6–8

Make this congee with just water if you like, but chicken stock gives it more depth of flavour. The stock will keep for up to 4 days in the fridge. I always love an extra dollop of XO sauce or chilli sauce on my congee. You can substitute the prawn meat with anything – duck, pork, crab, chicken or shredded vegetables.

200 g (7 oz/1 cup) jasmine rice
3 teaspoons sea salt
vegetable oil, for shallow frying
1 large knob fresh ginger, peeled
   and julienned
500 g (1 lb 2 oz) raw prawn (shrimp) meat,
   cut into bite-sized pieces
20 g (³/4 oz/¹/4 cup) crispy fried shallots
35 g (1¹/4 oz/¹/4 cup) roasted unsalted
   peanuts, lightly crushed
15 g (¹/2 oz/¹/4 cup) thinly sliced spring
   onions (scallions)
1 large handful coriander (cilantro) leaves
2 long fresh red chillies, thinly sliced
soy sauce, to serve

Fresh chicken stock
(makes about 2.5 litres/87 fl oz/10 cups)
1.6 kg (3 lb 8 oz) whole corn-fed
   free-range chicken

To make the stock, wash the chicken and remove the fat from the cavity. Set the chicken on a chopping board and use a large cook's knife or cleaver to cut off the legs at the point where the thigh and the drumstick meet. Make a few slashes into the flesh with a sharp knife. Cut off the wings where they meet the breast, then cut down the side of the chicken so the back comes off the breast. Cut the back and breast in half, and again, cut into the flesh slightly.

Put 3 litres (105 fl oz) water in a large saucepan and add the chicken pieces. Bring to the boil, then reduce the heat to the barest simmer and cook, uncovered, for about 4 hours. Remove any impurities from the surface during the cooking process. Carefully strain the stock twice through a fine strainer lined with muslin (cheesecloth) and discard the chicken pieces. Cool to room temperature, then refrigerate; remove the layer of fat before using.

Wash the rice in several changes of cold water. Put the rice in a large heavy-based saucepan with 1.5 litres (52 fl oz/6 cups) cold water and the sea salt. Leave to soak overnight at room temperature.

Drain off the soaking water, then add 2.5 litres (87 fl oz/10 cups) of the stock and bring the rice to the boil over high heat. Reduce the heat to a low simmer, cover and cook for 2 hours, checking from time to time to ensure the rice isn't sticking to the base. Add a little more stock or water as needed to achieve the desired consistency – some like congee quite thick, others prefer it runny.

Heat the vegetable oil in a small frying pan over high heat. When the oil is shimmering, add the ginger and immediately reduce the heat. Move the ginger around in the oil to evenly fry it, removing it from the oil when it begins to turn golden and crispy. Drain on some paper towel. Stir the fried ginger through the congee, then add the prawn meat and stir until it turns opaque.

Ladle the congee into four serving bowls. Garnish as desired using the fried shallots, peanuts, spring onions and coriander. Serve with a small dish of chilli and the soy sauce for everyone to add as they need. Don't add the soy sauce any earlier as it will spoil the pearl-white look of the congee.

Note
Crispy fried shallots are available in Asian supermarkets.

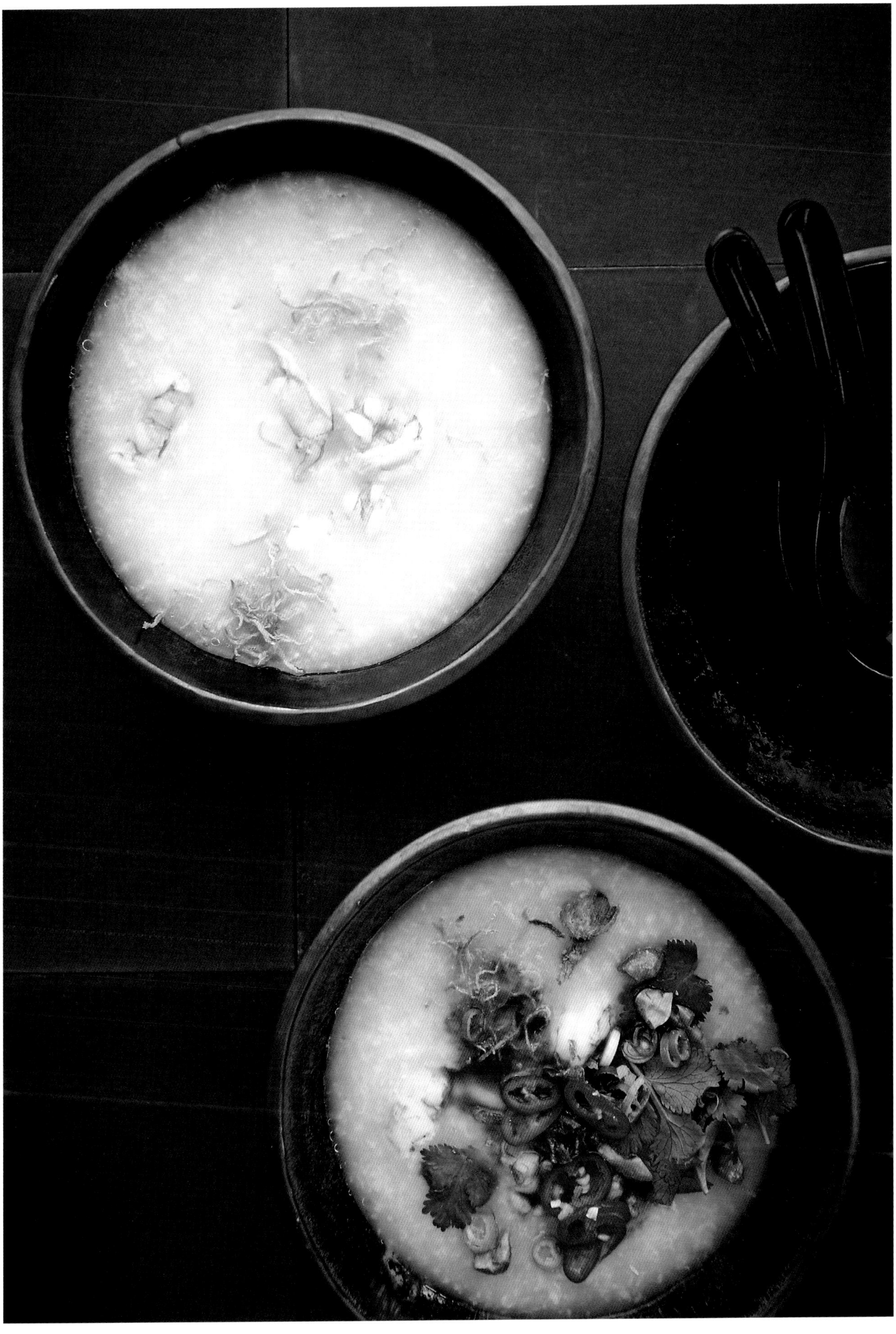

Spanish-style chorizo, saffron and chickpea soup

Serves 6–8

Use tinned chickpeas in this soup if you like; it will speed up the whole process. They won't need soaking or cooking – just rinse, drain and stir them in at the end to heat through.

95 g (3 1/4 oz / 1/2 cup) dried chickpeas, soaked overnight
1 tablespoon olive oil
2 chorizo sausages, cut into 1 cm (1/2 inch) pieces
2 garlic cloves, finely chopped
1 small red onion, finely diced
very small pinch of saffron threads
80 ml (2 1/2 fl oz / 1/3 cup) dry sherry
1.5 litres (52 fl oz / 6 cups) Fresh chicken stock (page 56)
1 large potato, peeled and cut into 1 cm (1/2 inch) pieces
1 small zucchini (courgette), cut into 1 cm (1/2 inch) pieces
500 g (1 lb 2 oz) English spinach, leaves roughly shredded
sea salt and freshly ground black pepper

Drain the chickpeas, rinse and place in a saucepan with plenty of fresh water. Bring to the boil over high heat, then reduce the heat to low and simmer for 45 minutes or until tender. Drain well.

Meanwhile, heat the olive oil in a saucepan over medium–high heat. Sauté the chorizo until golden, then transfer to a bowl and set aside.

Reduce the heat and add the garlic, onion and saffron to the same pan. Cook, stirring, until the onion has softened. Add the sherry and deglaze the pan, scraping the base with a wooden spoon. Add the stock and potato and bring to the boil. Reduce the heat and gently simmer for about 15 minutes. Add the zucchini and cook until tender.

Stir through the chickpeas, shredded spinach leaves and chorizo. Cook for a few minutes or until just heated through. Season to taste and serve immediately.

Fried eggplant with miso sauce

Serves 4

Instead of using large eggplants, you could try Japanese eggplants – split them lengthways down the middle, then mix all the other ingredients together and marinate the eggplants for a couple of hours before grilling them on a barbecue – they are so tasty.

2 dried red chillies
80 ml (2¹/₂ fl oz/¹/₃ cup) sake
60 ml (2 fl oz/¹/₄ cup) mirin
2 tablespoons Japanese soy sauce
75 g (2¹/₂ oz/¹/₃ cup) caster
　(superfine) sugar
100 g (3¹/₂ oz) red miso paste
125 ml (4 fl oz/¹/₂ cup) sesame oil
2 large eggplants (aubergines), cut into
　3 cm (1¹/₄ inch) cubes
1 handful coriander (cilantro) leaves,
　to serve

Crush the chillies in a mortar with a pestle.

Mix the sake, mirin, soy sauce and sugar together in a small bowl. In a separate bowl, mix the miso paste with 80 ml (2¹/₂ fl oz/¹/₃ cup) water to soften the paste.

Heat the sesame oil in a large frying pan over medium–high heat and add the crushed chillies to flavour the oil. When the oil is smoking, add the eggplant and fry for 8–10 minutes or until golden and tender. Reduce the heat, add the sake mixture and stir for 2–3 minutes. Add the miso and cook, stirring, for another couple of minutes.

Spoon the eggplant mixture onto a serving plate and garnish with the coriander leaves.

Spice-braised beef soup with hot bean paste

Serves 4

Be warned – this delicious soup *is* spicy, but you'll find it very satisfying. If you don't want to use noodles you could serve it with steamed rice – spoon the meat and some broth onto the rice, eat it and then drink the remaining broth.

700 g (1 lb 9 oz) beef brisket, trimmed
1 star anise
1 teaspoon sichuan peppercorns
1 teaspoon fennel seeds
1 cinnamon stick
80 ml (2^1/$_2$ fl oz/^{1}/$_3$ cup) vegetable oil
2 garlic cloves, thinly sliced
1 small knob of ginger, peeled and
    finely chopped
2 spring onions (scallions), thinly sliced
2 tablespoons gochujang (Korean hot
    bean paste)
2 tablespoons Chinese soy bean paste
1 tablespoon shaoxing rice wine
60 ml (2 fl oz/^{1}/$_4$ cup) light soy sauce
1 tablespoon caster (superfine) sugar
360 g (12^3/$_4$ oz) fresh shanghai noodles
3 Chinese cabbage (wong bok) leaves,
    cut into 3 cm (1^1/$_4$ inch) pieces
1 long fresh red chilli, thinly sliced
1 handful coriander (cilantro) leaves

Put the beef in a stockpot or very large saucepan with plenty of water, then bring to the boil. When scum rises to the top and the water is boiling, remove and rinse the beef. Discard the water and clean the pot. Cut the beef into 2 cm (^{3}/$_4$ inch) pieces.

Dry-fry the spices in a frying pan over medium heat for 4–5 minutes or until fragrant. Allow to cool, then wrap in a piece of muslin (cheesecloth) and tie with kitchen string to make a spice bag that is easy to remove from the soup.

Return the beef to the clean pot with the spice bag and 2.5 litres (87 fl oz/10 cups) water. Bring to the boil, then reduce the heat and simmer for 1^1/$_2$ hours or until tender. Lift out the beef and the spice bag. Reserve the stock, beef and spice bag.

Heat the oil in a wok over high heat. Stir-fry the garlic, ginger and spring onions in the hot oil for 1 minute. Add both of the bean pastes and cook until fragrant. Deglaze the wok with the shaoxing, then season with the soy sauce and sugar. Adjust the seasoning as needed. Add the beef pieces, spice bag and 1.25 litres (44 fl oz/5 cups) of the reserved stock. Bring to the boil, then reduce the heat to low and simmer for 15 minutes.

Meanwhile, cook the noodles in a saucepan of boiling salted water for 8–10 minutes or until al dente, then drain and set aside.

Add the cabbage to the soup and cook for a few minutes until tender, then add the noodles and cook until just heated through. Discard the spice bag.

Ladle the soup into four large, deep bowls and garnish with the chilli and coriander.

Fragrant broth with king prawns and udon noodles

Serves 6

I've used a beef brisket to make the broth, but you can use chicken or any type of seafood. You could also use dried udon or fresh egg noodles – there's always a great selection of fresh and dried noodles in Asian supermarkets.

Broth
500 g (1 lb 2 oz) beef brisket
3 litres (105 fl oz) Fresh chicken stock
    (page 56)
100 ml (3 1/2 fl oz) peanut oil
5 garlic cloves, sliced
1 large knob fresh ginger, peeled
    and thinly sliced
12 red Asian shallots, sliced
2 cinnamon sticks
3 star anise
1 teaspoon coriander seeds
1 1/2 tablespoons grated palm sugar
    (jaggery)
125 ml (4 fl oz / 1/2 cup) fish sauce

Marinated onion
1 small white onion, very thinly sliced
    into rounds
1 tablespoon sea salt
juice of 2 lemons

For the soup
6 spring onions (scallions), white part only,
    sliced into rounds
100 g (3 1/2 oz) coriander (cilantro) leaves
    and stems
600 g (1 lb 5 oz) fresh udon noodles,
    cooked as per directions on packet,
    drained
12 large cooked king prawns
    (shrimp), peeled, deveined
    and halved lengthways
freshly ground white pepper

To serve
mint leaves
Vietnamese mint leaves
sweet Thai basil leaves
bean sprouts
1 lemon, cut into 6 wedges
sriracha chilli sauce

To make the broth, put the brisket in a stockpot or very large saucepan with 5 litres (175 fl oz) water and bring to the boil. Boil vigorously for 10 minutes. Skim off all the scum and fat that rises to the top. Pour away the boiling water and wash the brisket carefully, removing all the bits of stuck-on protein and muck. Wash the pan and put the brisket back in. Pour in the chicken stock and bring to a simmer. Cook very gently for 30 minutes, skimming constantly.

Meanwhile, add the peanut oil to a hot wok. Fry the garlic, ginger and shallots separately over high heat until golden brown. Remove from the wok and drain on paper towel. Add these flavourings to the brisket stock after the first 30 minutes, then simmer for another 1 hour. Skim regularly, removing any excess oil.

Meanwhile, toast the cinnamon, star anise and coriander seeds in a dry frying pan until fragrant, watching to make sure they don't burn.

Tip the toasted spices on top of the stock and simmer for a further 1 1/2 hours. The stock should be very clear and full flavoured. Remove from the stove and pass through a fine strainer, then strain through a piece of muslin (cheesecloth). Season the broth with the palm sugar and fish sauce.

Meanwhile, to make the marinated onion, sprinkle the onion with the sea salt, place in a colander over a bowl and stand for 30 minutes. Rinse, then pat dry and marinate the onion in the lemon juice.

Very thinly slice the brisket lengthways and keep it moist with a little of the broth until needed.

Divide the spring onions and coriander leaves among six bowls. Place the noodles, brisket and prawns on top. Pour over the hot broth and add a pinch of freshly ground white pepper.

Arrange the fresh herbs, bean sprouts, marinated onion, lemon wedges and chilli sauce on a central serving platter for diners to season their soup as they wish.

FRAGRANT BROTH WITH KING PRAWNS AND UDON NOODLES

Zucchini parmigiana

Serves 6

Parmigiana makes a delicious vegetarian main meal, but is also great as a side with roast beef or chicken.

1 kg (2 lb 4 oz) tomatoes
60 ml (2 fl oz/^{1}/$_4$ cup) extra virgin olive oil
1 brown onion, diced
sea salt and freshly ground black pepper
4 garlic cloves, chopped
1 handful oregano leaves
4 large free-range eggs
125 ml (4 fl oz/^{1}/$_2$ cup) milk
150 g (5^1/$_2$ oz/1 cup) plain
      (all-purpose) flour
olive oil, for shallow frying and brushing
6 large zucchini (courgettes), sliced
      lengthways about 3 mm (^{1}/$_8$ inch) thick
200 g (7 oz/2 cups) finely grated
      parmesan cheese
200 g (7 oz) mozzarella cheese, sliced
15 g (^{1}/$_2$ oz/^{1}/$_2$ cup) loosely packed basil
      leaves, torn
70 g (2^1/$_2$ oz/1 cup) roughly chopped
      stale sourdough bread

Score the base of each tomato and blanch in a saucepan of boiling water for 30–60 seconds. Remove with a slotted spoon and plunge into ice-cold water. Peel away the skins, cut the tomatoes into quarters and scrape out the seeds, then roughly chop the flesh.

Heat 2 tablespoons of the extra virgin olive oil in a frying pan over medium heat. Add the onion and sea salt and sauté until soft, then add half the garlic and cook until golden – be careful not to burn the garlic. Add the tomatoes and half the oregano and season with black pepper. Simmer over medium heat for 20 minutes or until the tomatoes have collapsed and you have a thick sauce. Set aside.

Whisk together the eggs and milk and season with salt and pepper. Place the flour in a shallow bowl and season. Heat the olive oil for shallow frying in a large frying pan over medium heat. Working in batches, lightly flour the zucchini slices, shaking away the excess, then dip in the egg mixture and put straight in the frying pan. Cook until golden on both sides, then drain on paper towel.

Preheat the oven to 180°C (350°F). Brush a 2.5 litre (87 fl oz/10 cup) ovenproof dish with oil. Layer some of the tomato sauce on the bottom of the dish and top with a layer of zucchini, then a layer of parmesan, mozzarella and basil. Repeat until all the ingredients are used, finishing with a layer of tomato sauce and parmesan. Bake for 40 minutes or until the top is golden.

Meanwhile, put the chopped sourdough, remaining garlic and a little sea salt in a food processor and chop to form breadcrumbs. Heat the remaining 1 tablespoon extra virgin olive oil in a frying pan over low heat. Stir the breadcrumbs until golden and crisp, then remove from the heat and set aside to cool. Roughly chop the remaining oregano and mix through the breadcrumbs.

Garnish the parmigiana with the crispy breadcrumbs and serve.

ZUCCHINI PARMIGIANA

Vegetable tagine

Serves 4

Delicious served with couscous and roasted wedges of pumpkin (squash). You will only need half the chermoula here, so refrigerate the rest to use in another recipe such as the Duck, olive and date tagine (page 154) or the Tagine of king prawns, chickpeas, almonds and cherry tomatoes (page 128).

4 large tomatoes
2 tablespoons olive oil
2 large red onions, cut into wedges
2 teaspoons sea salt
4 carrots, peeled and thickly sliced on the diagonal
8 celery stalks, thickly sliced
2 red capsicums (peppers), cut into strips
1 x 400 g (14 oz) tin chickpeas, rinsed well and drained
2$^{1}/_{2}$ tablespoons honey
60 ml (2 fl oz/$^{1}/_{4}$ cup) lemon juice
90 g (3$^{1}/_{4}$ oz/$^{1}/_{2}$ cup) Ligurian olives
1 small handful coriander (cilantro) leaves
1 small handful flat-leaf (Italian) parsley leaves

Chermoula
(makes 500 ml/17 fl oz/2 cups)
1 red onion, roughly chopped
4 garlic cloves, roughly chopped
70 g (2$^{1}/_{2}$ oz/$^{1}/_{2}$ bunch) flat-leaf (Italian) parsley, including stems, roughly chopped
40 g (1$^{1}/_{2}$ oz/$^{1}/_{2}$ bunch) coriander (cilantro), including stems, roughly chopped
1 tablespoon ground cumin
1 tablespoon ground turmeric
1 tablespoon chilli powder, or to taste
2 teaspoons sweet paprika
1 teaspoon sea salt
150 ml (5 fl oz) extra virgin olive oil
juice of 1 lemon

To make the chermoula, add all the ingredients to a blender and blend until the mixture forms a paste.

Score the base of each tomato and blanch in a saucepan of boiling water for 30–60 seconds. Remove with a slotted spoon and plunge into ice-cold water. Peel away the skins, cut the tomatoes into quarters and scrape out the seeds, then roughly chop the flesh.

Heat the olive oil in a large heavy-based saucepan. Add the onions and sea salt and cook over medium heat until slightly softened. Add half the chermoula paste and cook, stirring, for 2 minutes or until fragrant and the raw flavour of the spices is cooked out. Stir through the carrots, celery, capsicums, tomatoes and 500 ml (17 fl oz/2 cups) water. Cover and cook over low heat for about 20 minutes.

Stir the chickpeas into the tagine, then replace the lid and cook for a further 25 minutes or until the vegetables are tender. Stir in the honey, lemon juice and olives.

Spoon the tagine into a large bowl, garnish with the coriander and parsley leaves and serve.

A great salad will always have contrasting textures, fresh flavours and brilliant bursts of colour.

Green mango salad

Serves 4

You should be able to find all of the ingredients for this salad in an Asian supermarket. Scud chillies are hot, very small, wild green chillies used in South-East Asian cooking. Invest in a mandolin or julienne grater to make light work of slicing the mangoes and shallots.

150 g (5 1/2 oz) snake (yard-long) beans,
    cut into 3 cm (1 1/4 inch) lengths
35 g (1 1/4 oz / 1/4 cup) roasted peanuts
2 tablespoons dried shrimp (optional)
120 g (4 1/4 oz) cherry tomatoes, halved
2 green mangoes, julienned
2 small French shallots, very thinly sliced
15 g (1/2 oz / 1/2 cup) coriander
    (cilantro) leaves

Dressing
2 garlic cloves, chopped
2 long fresh red chillies, chopped
2 tablespoons grated light palm sugar
    (jaggery)
60 ml (2 fl oz / 1/4 cup) fish sauce
60 ml (2 fl oz / 1/4 cup) lime juice
1 fresh scud chilli, finely chopped
    (optional)

Blanch the snake beans in boiling water until al dente, about 2 minutes. Refresh in iced water, then drain well.

Crush the peanuts in a mortar with a pestle, then place in a large mixing bowl. If you are using the shrimp, pound them, then add to the bowl. Pound the snake beans, then very lightly pound the tomatoes and add both to the bowl.

To make the dressing, pound the garlic in the mortar with the pestle, then add the red chillies. Pound together, then add the palm sugar, fish sauce, lime juice and scud chilli, if using. Mix together until thoroughly combined and the sugar has dissolved. Taste and adjust as needed.

Add the dressing to the bean mixture along with the green mangoes, shallots and coriander leaves. Mix thoroughly and present on a large serving platter.

Note
You can substitute snake beans with green beans if you wish.

GREEN MANGO SALAD

Salad of farro with baby beetroot, gorgonzola and candied walnuts

Serves 4

Farro is a grain that is low in gluten and has a wonderful nutty flavour. If you don't like blue cheese, ricotta is a great substitute for the gorgonzola dolce, or crumble some feta through the salad for a slightly stronger taste.

1 kg (2 lb 4 oz/2 bunches) baby beetroot
60 ml (2 fl oz/^{1}/$_{4}$ cup) red wine vinegar
125 g (4^{1}/$_{2}$ oz/^{2}/$_{3}$ cup) light brown sugar
2 bay leaves
160 g (5^{1}/$_{2}$ oz) farro
100 g (3^{1}/$_{2}$ oz) gorgonzola dolce
1 small handful dill sprigs

Candied walnuts
95 g (3^{1}/$_{4}$ oz/^{1}/$_{2}$ cup) walnut pieces
2 tablespoons caster (superfine) sugar
vegetable oil, for deep-frying

Dressing
125 ml (4 fl oz/^{1}/$_{2}$ cup) extra virgin olive oil
2 tablespoons balsamic vinegar
2 teaspoons caster (superfine) sugar
2 teaspoons dijon mustard
2 small garlic cloves, finely chopped
1 teaspoon sea salt
freshly ground black pepper

Trim the beetroot stalks, leaving 1 cm (^{1}/$_{2}$ inch) attached. Wash thoroughly, then add the unpeeled beetroot to a saucepan with the red wine vinegar, brown sugar and bay leaves. Cover with water and bring to the boil. Reduce the heat and simmer until just tender, about 20 minutes (depending on the size of the beetroot). Drain the beetroot and set aside until cool enough to handle, then cut off the ends and peel off the skin. Cut the beetroot into halves or quarters if large.

Bring a saucepan of salted water to the boil. Add the farro and return to the boil, then reduce the heat to low and cook for 10–15 minutes or until tender. Drain and set aside to cool.

To make the candied walnuts, blanch the walnuts in boiling water, then immediately drain and toss in the caster sugar, shaking away the excess. Heat the vegetable oil in a large heavy-based saucepan or deep-fryer to about 180°C (350°F) or until a small cube of bread browns in 15 seconds. Deep-fry the walnuts for about 1 minute or until caramelised. Remove and set aside on paper towel to cool.

To make the dressing, whisk all of the ingredients together.

Combine the beetroot, farro, crumbled gorgonzola dolce, dill and candied walnuts with the dressing and gently toss together. Divide the salad among four plates and serve immediately.

SALAD OF FARRO WITH BABY BEETROOT, GORGONZOLA AND CANDIED WALNUTS

Radicchio, rocket, walnut and apple salad

Serves 6

This simple salad is also super delicious served with a dollop of mayonnaise on top – mix it through for that traditional Waldorf salad flavour.

$^1/_2$ head radicchio
$^1/_2$ frisée lettuce
1 head witlof (chicory)
$^1/_2$ green butter lettuce
squeeze of lemon juice
2 small granny smith apples
80 g (2$^3/_4$ oz) baby rocket (arugula)
60 g (2$^1/_4$ oz/$^1/_2$ cup) lightly toasted walnuts, roughly chopped
80 g (2$^3/_4$ oz/$^1/_2$ cup) lightly toasted pine nuts

Dressing
160 ml (5$^1/_4$ fl oz) extra virgin olive oil
2 tablespoons balsamic vinegar
sea salt and freshly ground black pepper

Separate all the lettuces into leaves, then wash and spin dry or drain very well. Tear any larger leaves into bite-sized pieces.

Prepare a bowl of water with a squeeze of lemon juice. Peel and core the apples and add them to the acidulated water to prevent them from discolouring. Thinly slice the apples, returning them to the water as you work.

To make the dressing, whisk the olive oil, balsamic vinegar and seasoning together.

Combine all of the leaves and nuts in a large bowl. Drain the apple slices well and add them to the salad along with enough of the dressing to lightly coat the leaves. Gently toss together, transfer to a large salad bowl and serve immediately.

RADICCHIO, ROCKET, WALNUT AND APPLE SALAD

Fennel and orange salad

Serves 4

Use blood oranges when they're in season or add some shaved raw globe artichokes.

1 large fennel bulb, halved lengthways
    and thinly sliced
3 baby red radishes, thinly sliced
2 oranges, rind and white pith removed,
    sliced into rounds
1 large avocado, quartered and sliced
seeds of $1/2$ pomegranate
2 tablespoons dill sprigs (optional)

Orange dressing
2 tablespoons orange juice
1 tablespoon lemon juice
2 tablespoons extra virgin olive oil
sea salt and freshly ground black pepper

To make the dressing, whisk the orange and lemon juices together in a small bowl with the olive oil until well combined. Season to taste.

Add the fennel, radishes, orange slices, avocado, pomegranate seeds and dill sprigs, if using, to a large bowl. Pour over the dressing and gently toss together to coat. Serve immediately.

FENNEL AND ORANGE SALAD

Warm salad of roast cauliflower, labna, green olives and almonds

Serves 4

It's easy to make your own labna – spoon some plain yoghurt into a strainer lined with muslin (cheesecloth) and suspend it over a bowl in the fridge for several hours or overnight, allowing the excess whey to drain away.

500 g (1 lb 2 oz) cauliflower florets
1 tablespoon extra virgin olive oil
sea salt and freshly ground white pepper
60 g (2 1/4 oz) natural almonds
120 g (4 1/4 oz) labna
125 g (4 1/2 oz/1 cup) green olives,
    pitted and sliced
20 g (3/4 oz) currants
1 teaspoon finely grated lemon zest
2 tablespoons flat-leaf (Italian) parsley
    leaves, chopped

Dressing
1 tablespoon lemon juice
60 ml (2 fl oz/1/4 cup) extra virgin olive oil
sea salt and freshly ground white pepper

Preheat the oven to 220°C (425°F). Put the cauliflower florets in a roasting tin and toss with the olive oil, a pinch of sea salt and a grind of white pepper. Roast for 15–20 minutes, turning halfway through, until the cauliflower is golden brown but still holding its shape. Set aside.

Reduce the oven to 180°C (350°F). Place the almonds on a baking tray in a single layer and roast, checking regularly, for 8–10 minutes or until golden. Set aside to cool, then roughly chop.

To make the dressing, whisk the lemon juice with the olive oil and season to taste.

Spread the labna over the base of four serving plates. Transfer the warm cauliflower to a bowl and toss with the roasted almonds, olives, currants, lemon zest, parsley and the dressing. Spoon the cauliflower mixture onto the labna and serve immediately.

WARM SALAD OF ROAST CAULIFLOWER, LABNA, GREEN OLIVES AND ALMONDS

Spinach, pea and broccolini salad with soft goat's cheese

Serves 4

If peas aren't in season, use frozen ones – most of the year they will be sweeter than fresh ones. I like to add baby cos (romaine) lettuce for its crisp texture if lamb's lettuce is hard to find. Use a dollop of garlic-flavoured yoghurt instead of the goat's cheese for a change. Serve the salad with some crusty bread for a light lunch or alongside some grilled meat, chicken or seafood for a more substantial meal.

400 g (14 oz) fresh peas in the pod
350 g (12 oz) broccolini, trimmed
50 g (1 3/4 oz) lamb's lettuce (corn salad)
50 g (1 3/4 oz) baby English spinach
1 handful mint leaves
100 g (3 1/2 oz) ashed goat's cheese, crumbled

Dressing
125 ml (4 fl oz / 1/2 cup) extra virgin olive oil
2 tablespoons red wine vinegar
sea salt and freshly ground black pepper

Remove the peas from the pods. Bring a large saucepan of salted water to the boil. Blanch the broccolini until al dente, about 4 minutes. Remove with a slotted spoon and refresh in iced water. Return the water to the boil and blanch the peas until al dente, about 3–5 minutes. Drain and refresh in iced water. Drain the vegetables well. Cut the broccolini on the diagonal into bite-sized pieces.

Cut the roots off the lamb's lettuce. Thoroughly wash and dry the lamb's lettuce, spinach and mint leaves. Roughly tear the mint leaves.

To make the dressing, whisk all the ingredients together in a bowl.

Put the broccolini, peas, lamb's lettuce, spinach, mint, dressing and goat's cheese in a large bowl and gently toss to combine. Serve on a platter or in a large salad bowl.

SPINACH, PEA AND BROCCOLINI SALAD WITH SOFT GOAT'S CHEESE

Warm salad of haloumi, grapes, olives and pomegranate with lemon vinaigrette

Serves 4

All of these wonderful flavours together make for a very exciting salad. I do love warm haloumi, but this salad is also great at room temperature using crumbled feta instead.

120 g (4^1/$_4$ oz) seedless flame grapes, on the vine
seeds of ^{1}/$_2$ pomegranate
40 g (1^1/$_2$ oz/^{1}/$_3$ cup) pitted Ligurian olives
40 g (1^1/$_2$ oz) baby rocket (arugula)
1 small handful mint leaves
1 tablespoon extra virgin olive oil
350 g (12 oz) haloumi cheese, thickly sliced
2 teaspoons za'atar

Lemon vinaigrette
1 tablespoon lemon juice
60 ml (2 fl oz/^{1}/$_4$ cup) extra virgin olive oil
sea salt and freshly ground black pepper

To make the lemon vinaigrette, whisk the lemon juice, olive oil and seasoning together.

Remove the grapes from the vine, wash and cut in half. Place in a bowl with the pomegranate seeds, olives, rocket and mint.

Heat the olive oil in a non-stick frying pan over high heat. Pan-fry the haloumi for 1 minute on each side or until golden.

Add the vinaigrette to the salad and toss to combine. Divide the salad and haloumi among four serving plates and sprinkle with the za'atar. Serve immediately.

Note
Za'atar is a Middle Eastern ground spice blend that typically contains dried thyme, sumac and sesame seeds.

WARM SALAD OF HALOUMI, GRAPES, OLIVES AND POMEGRANATE WITH LEMON VINAIGRETTE

Salad of fresh figs with walnuts, goat's curd and pomegranate vinaigrette

Serves 4

Beautiful just as it is, or you could dial up the texture and flavour by adding a couple of slices of prosciutto to each plate – who doesn't love figs and prosciutto together?

40 g (1^1/$_2$ oz) wild rocket (arugula)

1 small handful basil leaves, torn if large

30 g (1 oz/^{1}/$_4$ cup) lightly toasted walnuts, roughly chopped

6 fresh figs, at room temperature

70 g (2^1/$_2$ oz) goat's curd

Pomegranate vinaigrette

60 ml (2 fl oz/^{1}/$_4$ cup) extra virgin olive oil

2 teaspoons pomegranate molasses

^{1}/$_2$ teaspoon dijon mustard

1 French shallot, finely diced

sea salt and freshly ground black pepper

To make the vinaigrette, whisk the olive oil, pomegranate molasses, mustard, shallot and seasoning together.

Toss the rocket, basil and walnuts with half of the vinaigrette in a bowl. Arrange on a serving platter.

Cut the figs lengthways into quarters and arrange on top of the salad. Dollop spoonfuls of the goat's curd over the salad and drizzle with the remaining vinaigrette. Serve immediately.

SALAD OF FRESH FIGS WITH WALNUTS, GOAT'S CURD AND POMEGRANATE VINAIGRETTE

Seared tuna salad with sesame dressing

Serves 4

Shichimi togarashi is a Japanese spice mix. There are lots of different blends, so check out your local Asian supermarket and find one you like the best. This salad is also really good with seared prawns (shrimp) or scallops.

400 g (14 oz) piece fresh tuna (or sashimi tuna already cut into logs)
1 tablespoon shichimi togarashi
2 tablespoons olive oil
1 small Chinese cabbage (wong bok) heart, finely shredded
4 spring onions (scallions), sliced
2 carrots, cut into matchsticks
20 g ($^3/_4$ oz/$^2/_3$ cup) coriander (cilantro) leaves
40 g ($1^1/_2$ oz/$^1/_4$ cup) toasted pine nuts
2 tablespoons toasted sesame seeds

Sesame dressing
$1^1/_2$ tablespoons Chinese sesame seed paste
60 ml (2 fl oz/$^1/_4$ cup) light soy sauce
$2^1/_2$ tablespoons rice vinegar
$1^1/_2$ tablespoons caster (superfine) sugar
4 garlic cloves, finely chopped
2 tablespoons finely grated fresh ginger
60 ml (2 fl oz/$^1/_4$ cup) sesame oil

Cut the tuna into logs. Roll each piece in the shichimi togarashi. Heat the olive oil in a frying pan over medium–high heat. Sear the tuna until it is golden all over but the centre is still raw, about 30 seconds on each side. Transfer to a plate and allow to cool in the fridge while you prepare the other ingredients.

To make the dressing, mix the sesame paste and soy sauce together in a bowl. Add the vinegar and sugar, stirring to combine and dissolve the sugar. Whisk in the garlic, ginger and sesame oil. Thin the dressing with about 2 tablespoons water, until it is thin enough to easily coat the salad. Set aside for 30 minutes to allow the flavours to develop.

Combine the cabbage, spring onions, carrots and coriander in a bowl with the pine nuts and sesame seeds.

Cut the tuna into 5 mm ($^1/_4$ inch) slices. Dress the salad, then divide among four plates, top with the tuna slices and serve immediately.

SEARED TUNA SALAD WITH SESAME DRESSING

Always cook dried pasta al dente (meaning 'to the tooth', or firm) – this is usually a minute less than the instructions on the packet advise. Remember that fresh pasta cooks much more quickly. It's worth paying attention to the cooking time, as the texture is so important for the pasta to remain the hero of the dish.

Farfalle with beans, fennel and sausage

Serves 4

I often use pork and fennel sausages for this dish, in which case I leave out the fennel seeds. This can be made with any short pasta you like.

2 tablespoons extra virgin olive oil

3 Italian sausages, skin removed

2 small fennel bulbs, halved and thinly sliced, fronds reserved

2 brown onions, finely diced

8 garlic cloves, chopped

$1/2$ teaspoon fennel seeds (optional, see above)

1.4 litres (49 fl oz) Fresh chicken stock (page 56)

2 x 400 g (14 oz) tins chopped Italian tomatoes

1 x 400 g (14 oz) tin cannellini beans, rinsed and drained

1 large handful flat-leaf (Italian) parsley, finely chopped

250 g (9 oz) dried farfalle

40 g ($1^1/2$ oz) finely grated parmesan cheese

Heat the olive oil in a large heavy-based saucepan over medium heat. Add the sausages, breaking them up with a wooden spoon, and stir until golden. Add the sliced fennel, onions, garlic and fennel seeds, if using, and sauté until soft and fragrant. Pour in the chicken stock and tomatoes. Bring to the boil, then reduce the heat and simmer for 30–40 minutes or until thickened to a saucy consistency. Remove from the heat and stir through the cannellini beans and parsley.

Meanwhile, bring a saucepan of salted water to the boil, add the pasta and cook until al dente, a minute or so less than the packet directions. Drain the pasta, reserving some of the cooking liquid.

Immediately return the pasta to the pan, pour in the sauce and some of the reserved cooking water if needed and toss until combined. Sprinkle the pasta with the parmesan and chopped fennel fronds and serve immediately.

FARFALLE WITH BEANS, FENNEL AND SAUSAGE

Spaghettini with pangrattato, lemon and olive oil

Serves 4

'Pangrattato' is basically Italian for breadcrumbs – but sounds much more romantic! This is the simplest of pasta sauces and one I often cook at home. Because the main player is the pasta, choose a good-quality one. It is so important to cook the pasta only until al dente – the texture is as important as the taste. It's good to use sourdough that is a day or two old for the crumbs and, I hate to say it, good bread makes good crumbs. There is no substitute for freshly grated quality parmesan here; if you use pre-grated packaged stuff you might as well not cook the dish!

400 g (14 oz) dried spaghettini
80 ml (2 1/2 fl oz / 1/3 cup) extra virgin olive oil, plus extra to serve
60 g (2 1/4 oz / 1 cup) fresh breadcrumbs
1 teaspoon chilli flakes
sea salt and freshly ground black pepper
6 garlic cloves, chopped
1 large handful flat-leaf (Italian) parsley, finely chopped
grated zest and juice of 1 lemon
grated parmesan cheese, to serve

Bring a large saucepan of salted water to the boil, add the spaghettini and cook until al dente, a minute or so less than the packet directions.

Meanwhile, add the olive oil to a frying pan. Warm it to medium–hot but not smoking. Add the breadcrumbs, chilli flakes and a sprinkle of sea salt and sauté for about 5 minutes or until the breadcrumbs are golden. Add the garlic and cook for another minute, toss in the parsley and remove from the heat, then fold through the lemon zest. Season to taste with black pepper and a little more sea salt, then tip the crumbs into a large serving bowl.

Drain the pasta, reserving some of the cooking liquid. Immediately add the pasta to the crumbs with the lemon juice and a little extra olive oil. Toss to combine, adding some of the reserved cooking water if needed. Serve immediately with lots of grated parmesan.

SPAGHETTINI WITH PANGRATTATO, LEMON AND OLIVE OIL

Strozzapreti pasta with roasted pumpkin, marinated feta and pine nuts

Serves 4

Strozzapreti means 'priest choker' in Italian and it refers to a pasta shape that resembles a rolled towel with 's'-shaped ends. This short, twisted pasta is not as common as penne or macaroni but has tremendous visual appeal on the plate.

600 g (1 lb 5 oz) peeled pumpkin (squash), cut into large dice
80 ml (2$^{1}/_{2}$ fl oz/$^{1}/_{3}$ cup) extra virgin olive oil, plus extra to serve
1 teaspoon thyme leaves
sea salt and freshly ground black pepper
1 red onion, halved and thinly sliced
2 garlic cloves, finely chopped
60 ml (2 fl oz/$^{1}/_{4}$ cup) dry white wine
150 g (5$^{1}/_{2}$ oz) baby English spinach
40 g (1$^{1}/_{2}$ oz/$^{1}/_{4}$ cup) toasted pine nuts
400 g (14 oz) dried strozzapreti
320 g (11$^{1}/_{4}$ oz) soft marinated feta cheese

Preheat the oven to 180°C (350°F). Put the pumpkin on a baking tray and drizzle with half the olive oil. Sprinkle with the thyme leaves, season with sea salt and toss to combine. Roast for 25–30 minutes or until the pumpkin is golden and tender.

Heat the remaining olive oil in a frying pan over low heat and add the onion, garlic and a pinch of sea salt. Cook for about 10 minutes or until the onion is soft, then pour in the wine and simmer for 30 seconds. Add the roasted pumpkin, spinach and pine nuts and season with sea salt and black pepper.

Meanwhile, bring a large saucepan of salted water to the boil, add the pasta and cook until al dente, a minute or so less than the packet directions. Drain the pasta, reserving some of the cooking liquid.

Immediately return the pasta to the pan and add the pumpkin mixture, feta, a little extra olive oil and some of the reserved cooking water if needed. Toss to combine, then serve immediately.

STROZZAPRETI PASTA WITH ROASTED PUMPKIN, MARINATED FETA AND PINE NUTS

Ricotta gnocchi with spring vegetables and sage burnt butter

Serves 4

Making your own fresh gnocchi is fun and you will love the result. It is also great with a simple tomato or cheese and cream sauce.

175 g (6 oz) fresh ricotta cheese, well drained

175 g (6 oz) ricotta salata (salted ricotta), grated

1 free-range egg plus 1 yolk

130 g (4 1/2 oz) tipo '00' flour, plus extra for kneading

1/3 nutmeg, finely grated

1/4 teaspoon sea salt, plus extra for cooking

2 tablespoons olive oil

2 small zucchini (courgettes), sliced into rounds

8 asparagus spears, sliced on an angle

80 g (2 3/4 oz / 1/2 cup) peas, thawed if frozen

80 g (2 3/4 oz) baby English spinach

100 g (3 1/2 oz) unsalted butter

10 g (1/4 oz / 1/2 bunch) sage leaves, roughly torn

1 tablespoon lemon juice

2 tablespoons finely grated parmesan cheese

Put both types of ricotta in a large bowl along with the egg and yolk and mix with a wooden spoon until just combined. Sift in the flour, nutmeg and sea salt. Gently stir to combine, then turn the mixture out onto a floured benchtop. Using the back of your hand, gently knead the mixture until it just comes together. Divide the dough into four portions and roll each portion into a thin log. Cut the logs into 2 cm (3/4 inch) pillows.

Bring a large saucepan of water to the boil and add a good handful of sea salt. Reduce the heat and gently simmer the gnocchi in batches for 2 minutes or until they float to the surface. Scoop them out with a slotted spoon, drain well and keep warm.

Heat half the olive oil in a large frying pan over high heat. Sauté the zucchini until golden brown but still holding its shape. Transfer to a plate and repeat with the asparagus. Heat the remaining oil in the pan, then add the gnocchi, peas and spinach and cook until the spinach has just wilted. Return the zucchini and asparagus to the pan.

Meanwhile, melt the butter in a smaller frying pan over medium heat and add the torn sage leaves. Fry until the butter begins to foam and turn nut-brown, then add the lemon juice and season with sea salt, then remove from the heat.

Divide the gnocchi and vegetables among four serving plates. Spoon the sage burnt butter over the top, sprinkle with the parmesan and serve immediately.

RICOTTA GNOCCHI WITH SPRING VEGETABLES AND SAGE BURNT BUTTER

Spaghettini with prawns, basil, parsley and pistachios

Serves 4

I find this a sublime combination of flavours. Another way to serve this is to chop the prawns and sauté them quickly, then serve with penne.

1 garlic clove
$1/2$ teaspoon sea salt
1 large handful basil leaves
1 large handful flat-leaf (Italian)
    parsley leaves
1 small handful mint leaves
75 g (2$1/2$ oz/$1/2$ cup) roasted
    unsalted pistachio nuts
1 tablespoon finely grated
    parmesan cheese
1 tablespoon lemon juice
60 ml (2 fl oz/$1/4$ cup) extra virgin olive oil
freshly ground black pepper
400 g (14 oz) dried spaghettini
500 g (1 lb 2 oz) peeled raw
    king prawns (shrimp)

In a mortar, pound the garlic and half the sea salt into a paste with a pestle. Add the basil, parsley and mint and continue to pound until the herbs break down and form a thick paste. Add half the pistachios and work them in well so the paste has a creamy texture. Roughly chop the remaining pistachios and stir through the paste with the parmesan, lemon juice and 2 tablespoons of the olive oil. Season with more salt if required and add a grind of black pepper.

Meanwhile, bring a large saucepan of salted water to the boil, add the spaghettini and cook until al dente, a minute or so less than the packet directions.

Place a heavy-based frying pan over high heat with the remaining olive oil. Pan-fry the prawns for 1 minute on each side, then season with the remaining $1/4$ teaspoon sea salt. Remove from the heat.

Drain the pasta, reserving some of the cooking liquid. Immediately tip the pasta back into the pan, add the herb paste, cooked prawns and some of the reserved cooking water if needed and toss to combine.

Tip onto a large, deep plate and serve immediately.

SPAGHETTINI WITH PRAWNS, BASIL, PARSLEY AND PISTACHIOS

Braised squid with spaghetti

Serves 4

Any type of pasta works with the squid. Here I've used spaghetti, but I also love it with risoni. I adore the meaty texture and flavour that braising gives the squid. Serve it with bread for mopping up the sauce. Use baby octopus in place of the squid for a treat.

125 ml (4 fl oz/^{1}/$_2$ cup) extra virgin olive oil

2 carrots, peeled, halved and sliced

1 leek, white part only, halved and sliced

1 brown onion, diced

3 garlic cloves, finely chopped

^{1}/$_2$ teaspoon chilli flakes

sea salt and freshly ground black pepper

450 g (1 lb) cleaned squid tubes, cut into
   1 cm (^{1}/$_2$ inch) strips

125 ml (4 fl oz/^{1}/$_2$ cup) red wine vinegar

500 ml (17 fl oz/2 cups) red wine

1 teaspoon salted baby capers, rinsed
   well and drained

1 large handful flat-leaf (Italian)
   parsley leaves

400 g (14 oz) dried spaghetti

Heat the olive oil in a heavy-based saucepan over medium heat, add the carrots, leek, onion, garlic, chilli flakes and a little sea salt, and sauté for about 5 minutes. Add the squid and cook for a further 5 minutes. Stir in the vinegar and wine and gently simmer for 1 hour. Add the capers and parsley and check the seasoning.

Just before the squid is cooked, bring a large saucepan of salted water to the boil, add the spaghetti and cook until al dente, a minute or so less than the packet directions. Drain the pasta, reserving some of the cooking liquid.

Immediately return the pasta to the pan, add the squid mixture and some of the reserved cooking water if needed, then toss to combine. Spoon into four bowls and serve immediately.

Oxtail ragù with pappardelle pasta

Serves 4

Traditionally served with pasta, ragù also goes brilliantly with fresh gnocchi and is really delicious in wintertime on cheesy, creamy polenta. For a different taste, serve it with pecorino cheese instead of the parmesan.

60 g (2 1/4 oz) unsalted butter
60 ml (2 fl oz / 1/4 cup) extra virgin olive oil
1 kg (2 lb 4 oz) oxtail, thickly sliced by your butcher
2 bacon rashers, finely chopped
1 celery stalk, finely diced
1 carrot, peeled and finely diced
1 small brown onion, finely diced
3 garlic cloves, finely chopped
sea salt and freshly ground black pepper
500 ml (17 fl oz / 2 cups) full-bodied red wine
2 x 400 g (14 oz) tins chopped Italian tomatoes
250 ml (9 fl oz / 1 cup) Fresh chicken stock (page 56)
400 g (14 oz) dried pappardelle
finely grated parmesan cheese, to serve

Preheat the oven to 180°C (350°F).

Heat the butter and olive oil in a large flameproof casserole dish over medium heat. Add the oxtail pieces, bacon, celery, carrot, onion, garlic and a little sea salt. Stir and sauté over low heat for 15 minutes. Increase the heat, pour in the wine and simmer until reduced by about half. Stir in the tomatoes and chicken stock, cover with baking paper and bring to the boil. Cover with foil, transfer to the oven and cook for 3–3 1/2 hours or until the oxtail is completely tender.

Remove the oxtail from the sauce. When cool enough to handle, remove the meat and discard the bones. Fold the meat back through the sauce, add a grind of black pepper and check the seasoning.

Meanwhile, bring a large saucepan of salted water to the boil, add the pasta and cook until al dente, a minute or so less than the packet directions. Drain the pasta, add to the ragù and gently toss together.

Using a pair of tongs, divide the pasta among four deep pasta bowls. Spoon the remaining sauce over the top, sprinkle with some freshly grated parmesan and serve immediately.

With seafood, buy the freshest possible and buy local: it's the only way to ensure its sustainability. Get to know and trust your fishmonger. Finally, don't overcook seafood: it's a delicate protein and can change from sublime to dry in less than a minute. Pay attention.

Korean-flavoured seafood stew

Serves 4

I've got my Korean flavours going again – get out the gochujang! This stew is spicy but not crazy, so if you like it hot, add a teaspoon of chilli flakes and the fire will be increased considerably. Any combination of seafood is good here, and the broth really loves a bowl of rice.

8 clams (vongole)

500 ml (17 fl oz/2 cups) Fresh chicken stock (page 56)

3 tablespoons gochujang (Korean hot bean paste)

2 tablespoons sake

3 garlic cloves, chopped

1 teaspoon sea salt

100 g (3 1/2 oz) daikon radish, peeled, halved lengthways and sliced

100 g (3 1/2 oz) salmon fillet, cut into bite-sized pieces

100 g (3 1/2 oz) blue-eye trevalla fillet, cut into bite-sized pieces

4 large raw king prawns (shrimp), peeled and deveined

200 g (7 oz) cleaned squid tube, cut into 3 cm (1 1/4 inch) pieces

100 g (3 1/2 oz) firm tofu, cut into 2 cm (3/4 inch) pieces

8 mussels, hairy beards removed, scrubbed clean

8 oysters, shucked and meat removed

150 g (5 1/2 oz/1/2 cup) kimchi, cut into 3 cm (1 1/4 inch) pieces

4 spring onions (scallions), julienned

Soak the clams in cold water for 15 minutes, then drain and rinse well.

Add the stock, gochujang, sake, garlic, sea salt and daikon to a large saucepan. Bring to the boil, then reduce the heat to a gentle simmer. Remove about 125 ml (4 fl oz/1/2 cup) of the broth and place in a small saucepan with a tight-fitting lid over low heat.

Add the fish to the large pan and gently poach for about 1 minute, then add the prawns and turn after 1 minute. Add the squid and cook for 1 minute longer – all of this should take 4–5 minutes. Just before finishing, add the tofu pieces just to heat through, but don't overcook the seafood.

Meanwhile, add the mussels and clams to the small pan and cook, covered, until they start to open. Add the oyster meat and poach to warm through – all of this should take about 4 minutes as well (discard any mussels and clams that don't open).

Spoon the shellfish and cooking liquid from the small pan into a large serving bowl. Add the rest of the seafood and pour over most of its cooking liquid. Add the kimchi, garnish with the spring onions and serve immediately.

Note

If the clams are packaged and prewashed there is no need to soak them – just remove them from the packet and rinse.

KOREAN-FLAVOURED SEAFOOD STEW

King prawn ball and shiitake hotpot

Serves 4

The Japanese seasonings used here are well worth tracking down in an Asian supermarket. Sansho is a relative of sichuan pepper; like sichuan, it's not a true pepper. It's slightly numbing but not as much as sichuan and has an earthy lemon tang. Shichimi togarashi is a wonderful blend of spices that will jazz up any dish. You can buy it or make it – the main ingredients are chilli, sansho, orange peel, black and white sesame seeds, ginger and nori.

$1/4$ Chinese cabbage (wong bok), sliced
200 g (7 oz) fresh shiitake mushrooms,
    stems removed, sliced
1 small handful coriander (cilantro) leaves,
    roughly chopped
shichimi togarashi (see above), to serve

Prawn balls

600 g (1 lb 5 oz) raw king prawn (shrimp)
    meat, coarsely chopped
1 small knob fresh ginger, peeled and
    finely grated
2 tablespoons sake
$1/4$ teaspoon sea salt
$1/2$ teaspoon chilli flakes
pinch of sansho pepper

Broth

1 litre (35 fl oz/4 cups) Fresh chicken
    stock (page 56)
60 ml (2 fl oz/$1/4$ cup) light soy sauce
125 ml (4 fl oz/$1/2$ cup) mirin
$1/2$ teaspoon sea salt

To make the prawn balls, put the prawn meat, ginger, sake, sea salt, chilli flakes and sansho pepper in a food processor and pulse until you have a coarse paste. Transfer the paste to a bowl and set aside.

Prepare the broth by combining the chicken stock, soy sauce, mirin and sea salt in a bowl.

Put the cabbage in a large stockpot or very large saucepan. Add the shiitake mushrooms, pour in the broth and place over medium–high heat. As the broth starts to come to the boil, scoop up tablespoons of the prawn paste and add them to the hotpot one at a time. Gently simmer until the prawn balls float to the surface, about 5–7 minutes.

Remove the pot from the heat and carefully transfer the contents to an Asian-style earthenware pot. Sprinkle with the coriander and shichimi togarashi and serve at the table.

KING PRAWN BALL AND SHIITAKE HOTPOT

Miso-crusted ocean trout with stir-fried brown rice and nori

Serves 4

A healthy way to make a very tasty meal with brown rice. Any fish goes well with the miso marinade, as do scallops or prawns (shrimp) or, if you want to go all out, lobster. Getting a nice caramelised crust on the fish is very important – it really adds a lovely complexity of flavour.

270 g (9 1/2 oz / 1 1/3 cups) brown rice
4 ocean trout fillets, about 150 g (5 1/2 oz)
    each, skin removed
2 tablespoons sunflower oil
sea salt
1 teaspoon sesame oil
2 teaspoons soy sauce
2 teaspoons toasted sesame seeds
2 spring onions (scallions), thinly sliced
    on the diagonal
coriander (cilantro) leaves, to serve
2 sheets toasted nori, torn into
    small pieces
lime wedges, to serve

Miso marinade
3 tablespoons white miso paste
2 tablespoons caster (superfine) sugar
2 1/2 tablespoons mirin
1 1/2 tablespoons sake

Cook the brown rice according to the packet directions, then spread out on a tray and allow to cool. Cover with plastic wrap and refrigerate until the rice is cold – overnight if possible.

To make the miso marinade, whisk together the miso paste, sugar, mirin and sake in a heatproof bowl. Sit the bowl over a saucepan of simmering water and whisk occasionally for 30 minutes or until the marinade has thickened to the consistency of honey. Set aside until completely cooled.

Coat the fish in the miso mixture and marinate for at least 30 minutes, turning halfway through the marinating time.

Heat half the sunflower oil in a non-stick frying pan over medium heat. Remove the fish from the marinade, add it to the pan and cook until the marinade slowly caramelises and creates a crust. Turn and cook on the other side until caramelised – the fish should still be a little rare in the middle. The cooking time should be about 5 minutes altogether, depending on the thickness of the fillets. Remove the fish from the pan and set aside somewhere warm to rest.

Meanwhile, heat the remaining sunflower oil in a wok over high heat. Add the chilled rice, along with a pinch of sea salt, and stir-fry until the edges are crispy. Fold in the sesame oil, soy sauce, sesame seeds and spring onions.

Spoon the rice onto four plates and place the fish next to the rice. Garnish with the coriander and nori, then serve with the lime wedges.

Barbecued seafood with gochujang butter sauce

Serves 4

This makes a great meal with some steamed rice, lettuce leaves, gochujang (Korean hot bean paste), kimchi and sliced onions. Sandwich the seafood and condiments between the lettuce and finish by spooning the sauce and leftovers on the rice – so tasty. Gochujang will keep in the fridge and is great added to stir-fries. I also like to add soy sauce, sugar, vinegar and sesame oil to make a wonderful dressing for seafood. Once you have it in the house you will be addicted.

12 clams (vongole)
2 Moreton Bay bugs (flat-head lobsters)
8 raw king prawns (shrimp), shells on
2 Hiramasa kingfish fillets or mahi mahi fillets, halved
8 meaty scallops, roe removed
sea salt
extra virgin olive oil, for drizzling
12 mussels, hairy beards removed, scrubbed clean

Gochujang butter sauce
150 g (5^1/$_2$ oz) unsalted butter, at room temperature
2 tablespoons gochujang (Korean hot bean paste)
2 tablespoons Korean soy sauce
2 tablespoons lime juice

Soak the clams in cold water for 15 minutes, then drain and rinse well.

Preheat a well-oiled and clean barbecue on high heat. Have a tray ready to hold all the seafood once each type is cooked.

Using a sharp knife, split the bugs in half lengthways and devein. Split the prawns in half lengthways and devein.

Season the bugs, prawns, fish and scallops with sea salt and drizzle with a little olive oil. Place the bugs and prawns on the barbecue, cut side down, along with the fish, scallops, mussels and clams. After 1 minute, turn the prawns and scallops, cook for another 1 minute, then remove from the barbecue. The bugs will take about 6 minutes; turn them halfway through. The mussels and clams are ready when the shells open, after 3–4 minutes (discard any that don't open). Grill the fish pieces on both sides until just cooked through, about 4 minutes. Keep the seafood somewhere warm while you quickly make the sauce.

To make the sauce, melt the butter in a small saucepan. Whisk in the gochujang, soy sauce and lime juice.

Divide up all the seafood, spoon over the sauce and serve.

Note
If the clams are packaged and prewashed there is no need to soak them – just remove them from the packet and rinse.

BARBECUED SEAFOOD WITH GOCHUJANG BUTTER SAUCE

Adobo-marinated blue-eye fillets

Serves 4

The adobo marinade makes more than you need here, but it will last for 5 days in the fridge, or you can freeze it for up to a month. Use it for marinating any meat, chicken or prawns (shrimp).

4 skinless blue-eye trevalla fillets
1 teaspoon sea salt
2 tablespoons extra virgin olive oil
1 lime, cut into wedges

Adobo marinade
4 dried ancho chillies, split and seeded
squeeze of orange juice
1 tablespoon distilled white vinegar
1 garlic clove
$1/4$ teaspoon sea salt
$1/4$ teaspoon caster (superfine) sugar
pinch of dried oregano
pinch of ground cumin

To make the adobo marinade, heat a heavy-based frying pan over medium–low heat. Dry-fry the chillies, turning them over and pressing down with tongs until they are fragrant, lightly browned and the skin starts to blister, about $1^1/2$ minutes. Transfer to a bowl, cover with plenty of hot water and soak for about 30 minutes or until soft.

Drain the chillies, reserving the soaking liquid. Add the chillies and about 60 ml (2 fl oz/$1/4$ cup) of the liquid to a blender with the remaining marinade ingredients. Blend until smooth, adding more of the soaking liquid if needed.

Pat the fish fillets dry with paper towel and season with the sea salt. Place in a shallow glass bowl with 80 ml ($2^1/2$ fl oz/$1/3$ cup) of the adobo marinade and turn to coat both sides. Cover and refrigerate for about 30 minutes.

Heat the olive oil in a heavy-based frying pan over medium heat. Add the fish and cook for about 2 minutes, then turn and cook for another 2–3 minutes or until just cooked through. Allow to rest in a warm place for 5 minutes.

Place the fish on serving plates, squeeze some lime juice over the top and serve immediately.

ADOBO-MARINATED BLUE-EYE FILLETS

Pan-fried john dory with parsley, garlic and pine nuts

Serves 4

Any white-fleshed fish is good for this dish. Just make sure the fillets aren't too thick as you want them to cook quite quickly. You can also buy the breadcrumbs instead of making them – Japanese panko breadcrumbs are good. It's worth seeking out good-quality anchovies from a specialist food purveyor – buy the best you can afford. The difference in quality and flavour will make the dish so much better.

2 thick slices sourdough bread, crusts removed, finely chopped
2 teaspoons thyme leaves, finely chopped
125 ml (4 fl oz/1/2 cup) extra virgin olive oil
sea salt and freshly ground black pepper
1 small handful flat-leaf (Italian) parsley leaves, finely chopped
1 garlic clove, finely chopped
4 anchovy fillets, finely chopped
40 g (1 1/2 oz/1/4 cup) toasted pine nuts
4 john dory fillets, about 200 g (7 oz) each
75 g (2 1/2 oz/1/2 cup) plain (all-purpose) flour
125 ml (4 fl oz/1/2 cup) dry white wine

Preheat the oven to 180°C (350°F). Put the chopped bread, thyme and 1 tablespoon of the olive oil in a bowl, season with sea salt and black pepper and toss to combine. Tip onto a baking tray and toast for 5–10 minutes or until golden brown. Set aside to cool.

Mix the parsley, garlic, anchovies and pine nuts in a bowl with another 1 tablespoon of the olive oil.

Season the fish with salt and pepper and lightly dust with the flour, shaking away the excess.

Heat the remaining olive oil over high heat in a heavy-based frying pan that has a tight-fitting lid. Add the fish to the pan and cook, uncovered, for 30 seconds on each side or until lightly golden. Pour in the wine, then add 125 ml (4 fl oz/1/2 cup) water. Add the parsley and pine nut mixture, cover and gently simmer for 1 minute to infuse the flavours.

Place the fish on four plates, spoon the sauce over the top and sprinkle with the crispy breadcrumbs. Serve immediately.

Roast whole rainbow trout with bacon and basil

Serves 2

Inspired by the classic French dish of trout and bacon, I promise you that the earthy flavour of freshwater fish and bacon is a match made in heaven.

Position a shelf in the centre of the oven and preheat the oven to 220°C (425°F).

Pat the fish dry with paper towel. Season the cavities with sea salt and black pepper, then put the orange slices and basil sprigs inside. Season the outside of the fish with salt and pepper. Cut the strips of bacon in half crossways so you have six shorter strips. Arrange the strips, slightly overlapping and at an angle, so they cover the body of each fish, leaving the tail and head exposed. Place the fish, side by side, on a wire rack inside a heavy-duty baking tray with a rim.

Roast the fish for about 20 minutes, depending on the thickness, or until the bacon is crisp and the flesh of the fish is opaque but still moist at the thickest part of the back (check by inserting a knife along the backbone of the fish at the thickest part and prying the top fillet away from the bone – it should come away easily but still be moist nearest the bone). An instant-read thermometer inserted in the thickest part of the fish should read 130–140°C (250–275°F).

2 whole rainbow trout, cleaned and gutted
sea salt and freshly ground black pepper
4 thin orange slices
4 leafy basil sprigs
3 thin- or medium-cut bacon rashers
60 ml (2 fl oz/¼ cup) orange juice

Transfer the fish to two serving plates. Pour off all but a few teaspoons of fat from the baking tray, being careful not to pour off any juices (different bacon releases varying amounts of fat, so you may have a lot or barely any). Pour the orange juice over the tray and scrape with a wooden spoon to combine the drippings and orange juice. Drizzle this sauce over the fish and serve.

Steamed mussels with fennel, garlic and chorizo

Serves 4

Grill some sourdough bread, rub it with garlic and drizzle it with olive oil, ready to dunk into the mussel sauce.

2 tablespoons extra virgin olive oil
120 g (4 1/4 oz) chorizo sausages, sliced
1 small brown onion, finely diced
4 garlic cloves, thinly sliced
1 teaspoon sea salt
1 baby fennel bulb, halved and
    thinly sliced
2 teaspoons smoked sweet paprika
250 ml (9 fl oz/1 cup) dry sherry
2 tablespoons tomato paste
    (concentrated purée)
2 x 400 g (14 oz) tins chopped
    Italian tomatoes
500 ml (17 fl oz/2 cups) Fresh chicken
    stock (page 56)
1 kg (2 lb 4 oz) mussels, hairy beards
    removed, scrubbed clean
2 tablespoons flat-leaf (Italian) parsley
    leaves, roughly chopped
60 ml (2 fl oz/1/4 cup) lemon juice
freshly ground black pepper

Heat the olive oil in a large heavy-based saucepan over medium heat. Fry the chorizo until golden, then remove and set aside.

Add the onion, garlic and sea salt to the pan and cook until the onion is starting to soften. Add the fennel and paprika and continue cooking until the fennel is soft.

Pour in the sherry and simmer until the liquid has reduced by half. Add the tomato paste, stir well and cook for a few minutes, then add the tomatoes and stock. Bring to the boil, then reduce the heat and gently simmer for 10 minutes. Return the chorizo to the pan and simmer for another 10 minutes.

Add the mussels to the sauce, cover and gently simmer until the mussels open, about 3–4 minutes (discard any that don't open). Remove from the heat and stir in the parsley, lemon juice and black pepper to taste.

Take the mussels to the table in the pan and serve immediately.

STEAMED MUSSELS WITH FENNEL, GARLIC AND CHORIZO

Snapper and fennel pies

Serves 4

We often have these pot pies on our Qantas menus but they are easy to make at home and super delicious. Use any fish you like or use a mixture of seafood, such as prawns (shrimp), scallops and mussels. You could easily make one large pie if you prefer – the cooking time would be about the same.

2 sheets frozen puff pastry, thawed
600 g (1 lb 5 oz) skinless snapper fillets,
    cut into 3 cm (1^1/$_4$ inch) pieces
1 free-range egg
1 tablespoon milk

Fennel and dill sauce
80 g (2 ^{3}/$_4$ oz) butter
1^1/$_2$ tablespoons extra virgin olive oil
1 leek, white part only, thinly sliced
1 fennel bulb, finely diced
1 garlic clove, finely chopped
sea salt and freshly ground white pepper
pinch of cayenne pepper
75 g (2^1/$_2$ oz/^{1}/$_2$ cup) plain
    (all-purpose) flour
60 ml (2 fl oz/^{1}/$_4$ cup) dry white wine
500 ml (17 fl oz/2 cups) milk, warmed
^{1}/$_2$ teaspoon dijon mustard
60 ml (2 fl oz/^{1}/$_4$ cup) thin (pouring) cream
finely grated zest of ^{1}/$_2$ lemon
1 small handful dill, roughly chopped
1 small handful flat-leaf (Italian) parsley
    leaves, finely chopped

Preheat the oven to 180°C (350°F).

You will need four large ramekins or individual ovenproof dishes. Using the ramekins or dishes as a guide, cut four rounds from the pastry about 1 cm (^{1}/$_2$ inch) larger than the ramekins. Using a 3 cm (1^1/$_4$ inch) cutter, cut out four small rounds and place these in the centre of the four large rounds. Refrigerate the pastry until needed.

To make the sauce, heat the butter and olive oil in a saucepan over low heat. Add the leek, fennel, garlic, a pinch of sea salt, white pepper and cayenne pepper and cook for 10 minutes or until the vegetables are soft. Stir in the flour and cook until the mixture bubbles and becomes grainy. Gradually pour in the wine, stirring constantly, then gradually stir in the warm milk. Continue stirring until the mixture bubbles and thickens slightly. Stir in the mustard, cream, lemon zest, dill and parsley, then check the seasoning.

Fold the fish through the sauce, then divide the mixture among the ramekins and top with the pastry, pressing around the edges to seal. Whisk the egg and milk together, then brush over the pastry. Pierce the top of each pie to allow the steam to escape.

Put the pies on a baking tray and bake for about 20 minutes or until the pastry is golden. Serve warm with a green salad.

Pan-fried salmon with pipi sauce

Serves 4

Salmon cooked this way is perfect with some crusty bread to mop up all the lovely juices and a very simple salad – finely shaved cabbage with raw fennel and a few fennel fronds, lemon juice and a grassy olive oil. Clams would work beautifully instead of pipis and you can swap the salmon with a great piece of ocean trout or snapper if you like.

500 g (1 lb 2 oz) pipis
4 garlic cloves, roughly chopped
1 small knob fresh ginger, peeled and roughly chopped
2 teaspoons toasted fennel seeds
1/2 teaspoon sea salt, plus extra to season
1/2 teaspoon smoked sweet paprika
1/2 teaspoon chilli flakes
4 salmon fillets, skin on, about 180 g (6 oz) each
1 tablespoon extra virgin olive oil
1 small red onion, halved and thinly sliced
2 smoky bacon or pancetta rashers, finely diced
250 ml (9 fl oz/1 cup) dry white wine
155 g (5 1/2 oz/1 cup) shelled fresh peas
250 ml (9 fl oz/1 cup) Fresh chicken stock (page 56)
60 g (2 1/4 oz) unsalted butter
freshly ground black pepper
1 small handful flat-leaf (Italian) parsley, roughly chopped
crusty bread, to serve

Soak the pipis in cold water for 15 minutes, then drain and rinse well.

Put the garlic, ginger, fennel seeds and sea salt in a mortar and pound with a pestle to form a rough paste. Add the paprika and chilli flakes and pound a little more; it doesn't have to be too fine. Set aside.

Season the salmon fillets with sea salt, then heat the olive oil in a deep frying pan over high heat. Add the salmon, skin side down, and cook for 5 minutes or until the skin is crisp and golden. Turn and cook for about 4 minutes longer; the salmon should still be a little rare in the middle. Remove and rest on a warm plate.

Reduce the heat under the pan slightly, add the onion and bacon and a little more sea salt and cook for 5 minutes or until the onion is just becoming soft. Stir in the spice paste and cook for a few minutes, then pour in the wine and simmer for 5 minutes or until reduced by about half.

Add the peas, stock and pipis to the pan and bring to the boil. Reduce the heat to a gentle simmer, cover and cook for about 3 minutes or until the pipis have just opened. Remove the lid and simmer to reduce the sauce a little if necessary, then stir in the butter until just melted (don't let the sauce boil again once you add the butter). Remove and discard any pipis that have not opened. Add a good grind of black pepper, stir in the parsley and check the seasoning, adding more salt if needed. Return the salmon to the pan, skin side up, and spoon over some of the pan juices.

This is a beautiful dish to serve at the table. Divide the salmon among four bowls, spoon the pan juices and pipis over the top and serve with crusty bread.

Note
If the pipis are packaged and prewashed there is no need to soak them – just remove them from the packet and rinse.

PAN-FRIED SALMON WITH PIPI SAUCE

Sauté of snapper with fresh tomato and olive sauce

Serves 4

A delicious sauce with any type of seafood, as well as roasted or sautéed chicken.

3 large ripe tomatoes

8 garlic cloves

4 snapper fillets, skin on, about 180 g (6 oz) each

sea salt and freshly ground black pepper

2 tablespoons extra virgin olive oil

100 g (3 1/2 oz) unsalted butter

50 ml (1 1/2 fl oz) red wine vinegar

12 black olives, pitted and roughly chopped

1 large handful flat-leaf (Italian) parsley leaves, finely chopped

Score the base of each tomato and blanch in a saucepan of boiling water for 30–60 seconds. Remove with a slotted spoon and plunge into ice-cold water. Peel away the skins, cut the tomatoes into quarters and scrape out the seeds, then roughly chop the flesh.

Add the garlic to a small saucepan of salted water and bring to the boil, then drain and refresh in cold water. Repeat the blanching and cooling steps – the garlic should be tender.

Dry the snapper fillets as well as you can with paper towel and season with sea salt.

Heat the olive oil and half the butter in a heavy-based frying pan over high heat until the butter is foaming and the pan is hot. Add the fish, skin side down, and cook for 5 minutes or until the skin is crisp and golden. Turn the fish over and add the garlic to the pan. Cook for 3 minutes or until the fish is about three-quarters cooked. Transfer the fish to a plate and keep warm.

Add the vinegar and deglaze the pan, then add the tomatoes, olives and a little sea salt. Simmer for 5 minutes, then add the remaining butter and whisk until it melts and forms a beautiful sauce. Add the parsley and some black pepper, then check the seasoning and add some more salt if needed.

Pour a little sauce onto each plate and place a piece of fish on top, skin side up. Serve immediately.

Tagine of king prawns, chickpeas, almonds and cherry tomatoes

Serves 4

Use any sweet–sour combo you like and any seafood or meat. I like to use sweet vegetables like pumpkin (squash), yam, carrots and parsnips. I also add brussels sprouts and half heads of radicchio to tagines. Feel free to add different nuts and dried fruits you like as well. Olives are always a welcome addition.

250 ml (9 fl oz / 1 cup) Chermoula (page 66)
juice of 1 lemon
2 tablespoons honey
8 small French shallots, peeled
1 teaspoon sea salt
1 kg (2 lb 4 oz) raw king prawns (shrimp), shells on
1 preserved lemon
10 cherry tomatoes, halved
300 g (10 1/2 oz) tinned chickpeas, rinsed and drained
40 g (1 1/2 oz / 1/4 cup) blanched almonds

Add 1 litre (35 fl oz / 4 cups) water, the chermoula, lemon juice, honey, shallots and sea salt to a tagine or large saucepan that will fit all the ingredients. Bring to the boil, then reduce the heat, cover and gently simmer for about 30 minutes.

Peel and devein the prawns. Cut the preserved lemon into quarters and remove the pith. Thinly slice the rind and add it to the tagine along with the prawns, tomatoes, chickpeas and almonds. Stir to combine. Gently simmer, uncovered, for 1–2 minutes or until the prawns are cooked through.

Remove the tagine from the heat and either divide among four bowls or serve in the middle of the table. Serve immediately.

TAGINE OF KING PRAWNS, CHICKPEAS, ALMONDS AND CHERRY TOMATOES

At the very least, buy free-range chicken, but if possible make it organic as well. It makes a big difference in flavour but, even more importantly, ensures the chicken has been treated humanely. The same goes for eggs. It's great to eat with a clear conscience.

Pan-fried chicken breasts with horseradish cream sauce

Serves 4

I really like this simple sauce with roast chicken as well. Just deglaze the roasting tin with the vermouth to make a really creamy, yummy gravy. It also works well with fish. I serve potatoes that have been boiled and then pan-fried with this dish as well as a simple green salad, boiled beans or Creamed spinach (page 214). It is also great with mac and cheese – super-rich but oh so good!

4 free-range chicken breasts, skin on, about 180 g (6 oz) each
sea salt
extra virgin olive oil, for brushing

Horseradish cream sauce
100 ml (3 1/2 fl oz) dry vermouth
sea salt and freshly ground black pepper
200 ml (7 fl oz) thin (pouring) cream
60 g (2 1/4 oz) chilled unsalted butter, chopped
1 large handful flat-leaf (Italian) parsley leaves, finely chopped
45 g (1 1/2 oz / 1/2 cup) finely grated fresh horseradish
1 lemon, halved

Remove the chicken from the fridge 1 hour before cooking and season liberally with sea salt.

Preheat the oven to around 70°C (150°F) so you can rest the chicken there once it's cooked.

Use a heavy-based frying pan that is large enough to fit all of the chicken breasts. Heat the frying pan over medium–high heat. Brush the chicken breasts with olive oil and place in the hot pan, skin side down. Cook for 5 minutes or until the skin is crisp and golden, then turn and cook for a further 4 minutes or until the chicken is just cooked through. Transfer the chicken to a plate and rest in the oven while you make the sauce.

To make the sauce, pour the vermouth into the frying pan and scrape the bottom well. Add a good pinch of sea salt, pour in the cream and cook for 2 minutes at a rapid boil. Reduce the heat and whisk in the butter. Remove from the heat, stir in the parsley and horseradish and season with black pepper and a squeeze of lemon juice.

Place the chicken breasts on four plates and pour a generous amount of sauce over the top. Serve immediately.

Note
You can use a good-quality preserved horseradish if fresh horseradish is not available.

PAN-FRIED CHICKEN BREASTS WITH HORSERADISH CREAM SAUCE

Barbecued chicken 'devil style' with salsa verde

Serves 8

'Devil style' refers to the heat but you can omit the chilli flakes and just season the chickens with plenty of black pepper if you don't want them too fiery. This method of cooking chicken is one of my favourites. I find the legs cook quicker when the chicken is flattened, so the breast and leg meat are cooked closer to the same time.

2 x 2 kg (4 lb 8 oz) whole free-range
    chickens, butterflied (see page 142)
3 lemons
125 ml (4 fl oz/^{1}/2 cup) extra virgin olive oil
sea salt and freshly ground black pepper
large pinch of chilli flakes

Salsa verde
60 g (2^1/4 oz) stale sourdough bread,
    crusts removed
60 ml (2 fl oz/^{1}/4 cup) milk
1 small handful flat-leaf (Italian) parsley,
    roughly chopped
2 teaspoons salted baby capers, rinsed
    well and drained
2 anchovy fillets
juice of 1 lemon
1 teaspoon sea salt
125 ml (4 fl oz/^{1}/2 cup) extra virgin olive oil
^{1}/2 hard-boiled egg, finely chopped
freshly ground black pepper

Place the chickens on a board, skin side up, and roll over with a rolling pin, leaning heavily to flatten the chickens. Put the chickens in a wide, deep roasting tin, skin side up, and squeeze the juice from two of the lemons over the top. Drizzle with half the olive oil, then season with sea salt, plenty of black pepper and chilli flakes. Cover and marinate at room temperature for 1 hour.

Meanwhile, to make the salsa verde, soak the bread in the milk for about 5 minutes, then add to a food processor along with the parsley, capers, anchovies, lemon juice and sea salt. Chop until well combined. With the motor running, gradually pour in the olive oil to emulsify. Stir in the egg and season with black pepper.

Preheat a barbecue on medium heat.

Squeeze the juice from the remaining lemon into a small bowl, whisk in the remaining olive oil and season to taste, using plenty of pepper.

Remove the chickens from the marinade and place, skin side down, on the barbecue grill. Cover and cook for about 15 minutes or until the skin is well browned. Turn over and continue to cook, brushing with the lemon mixture every 5 minutes, for another 25–35 minutes or until the juices run clear when the thigh is pierced with a sharp knife. Set the chickens aside to rest for 10 minutes.

Transfer the chickens to a chopping board. Cut off the legs, then cut in half at the thigh and drumstick joint. Cut the breast in half down the middle, then cut each half into two pieces so that each piece has about the same amount of meat.

Arrange the chicken pieces on a large platter and serve with the salsa verde alongside.

Fragrant poached chicken and lamb pilaf

Serves 4

I know it sounds crazy – chicken and lamb together – but trust me, the lamb flavouring the rice and the shredded chicken just work. To serve as part of a banquet, add minted yoghurt, tabouleh, hummus and some flatbread.

1 small brown onion, sliced
1 celery stalk, roughly chopped
2 cardamom pods, crushed
1 clove
1 cinnamon stick
1/2 teaspoon black peppercorns
sea salt
800 g (1 lb 12 oz) free-range double
    chicken breasts, bone in and skin on
80 g (2 3/4 oz/1/2 cup) toasted pine nuts
25 g (1 oz/1/4 cup) toasted flaked almonds
1 handful coriander (cilantro) leaves,
    finely chopped

Lamb pilaf
1 tablespoon extra virgin olive oil
40 g (1 1/2 oz) butter
1 small brown onion, finely diced
1 teaspoon sea salt
150 g (5 1/2 oz) lean minced (ground) lamb
1/4 teaspoon ground cinnamon
1/4 teaspoon ground allspice
1/4 teaspoon ground cumin
1/4 teaspoon ground coriander
200 g (7 oz/1 cup) long-grain rice,
    rinsed well

Put the onion, celery, whole spices and a pinch of sea salt in a saucepan. Add the chicken, skin side down, and enough water to cover. Bring to the boil, then reduce the heat and gently simmer for 6 minutes. Turn off the heat and leave the chicken in the hot stock for 20 minutes.

Remove the chicken from the stock. Strain the stock through a piece of muslin (cheesecloth) and set aside. When the chicken is cool enough to handle, discard the skin and bones and shred the meat into large bite-sized pieces.

To make the pilaf, heat the olive oil and butter in a large saucepan. Sauté the onion and sea salt over low heat for about 10 minutes or until the onion has softened. Increase the heat, add the lamb and cook until the juices have evaporated. Add the ground spices and rice and stir for a few minutes to coat the rice in the spices. Pour in 310 ml (10 3/4 fl oz/1 1/4 cups) of the reserved stock. Bring to the boil, then reduce the heat, cover and gently simmer for 10–12 minutes or until the rice is al dente and all the liquid has been absorbed.

Spoon the rice onto a platter and top with the shredded chicken, pine nuts, almonds and coriander. Serve immediately.

FRAGRANT POACHED CHICKEN AND LAMB PILAF

Chicken in crazy water

Serves 4

Crazy water is a classic Italian way to cook fish, but I find it also works really well with chicken. Cook this in summer when you can find the really ripe, tasty tomatoes that are crucial to the success of this dish.

6 large ripe tomatoes
3 large garlic cloves, thinly sliced
2 small fresh red chillies, seeded and chopped
60 ml (2 fl oz / 1/4 cup) extra virgin olive oil
1/2 teaspoon sea salt
1 large handful flat-leaf (Italian) parsley leaves, finely chopped
8 small boneless, skinless free-range chicken thighs

Score the base of each tomato and blanch in a saucepan of boiling water for 30–60 seconds. Remove with a slotted spoon and plunge into ice-cold water. Peel away the skins, cut the tomatoes into quarters and scrape out the seeds, then roughly chop the flesh.

Use a heavy-based frying pan that will fit the chicken thighs snugly. Put the tomatoes, garlic, chillies, olive oil, sea salt, most of the parsley and 875 ml (30 fl oz / 3 1/2 cups) water in the pan. Bring to the boil, then reduce to a gentle simmer, cover and cook for 45 minutes. Remove the lid, increase the heat and cook until the liquid has reduced by half.

Add the chicken thighs to the pan and gently simmer for 10 minutes, then turn and cook for a further 10 minutes or until the chicken is cooked through. Remove the pan from the heat and garnish with the remaining parsley.

Place two chicken thighs on each plate, spoon the sauce over the top and serve immediately.

Oven-baked tandoori chicken with mint and coriander relish

Serves 4 as part of a shared banquet

If the weather is nice enough to venture outside, the tandoori chicken is great when grilled on a super-hot barbecue. For best results, marinate it overnight before cooking. You can use chicken breasts, thighs or drumsticks, but I think the thighs have the best flavour, especially when grilled, and there's less chance of them drying out.

1 kg (2 lb 4 oz) skinless free-range chicken thighs (about 6), bone in

Marinade
1 small knob fresh ginger, peeled and finely grated
4 garlic cloves, finely chopped
1 tablespoon tandoori paste
2 teaspoons ground cumin
2 teaspoons ground coriander
1 teaspoon garam masala
1/2 teaspoon chilli powder
1/2 teaspoon ground turmeric
pinch of sea salt
200 g (7 oz/3/4 cup) plain yoghurt

Mint and coriander relish
30 g (1 oz/1 cup) coriander (cilantro) leaves
20 g (3/4 oz/1/4 cup) mint leaves
1/2 small brown onion, diced
2 garlic cloves
1 teaspoon finely grated fresh ginger
1 fresh green chilli, seeded and thinly sliced
1 tablespoon lemon juice
1/4 teaspoon cumin seeds
sea salt

To make the marinade, combine all the ingredients in a large bowl and mix well.

Make a few shallow incisions in the chicken thighs, then add to the marinade. Rub the marinade into the chicken and toss to coat well. Cover and refrigerate for at least 4–6 hours.

Remove the chicken thighs from the fridge and preheat the oven to 220°C (425°F).

Line a large roasting tin with foil and place a wire rack inside. Arrange the chicken pieces on the rack so they are not touching each other. Roast the chicken for 20–25 minutes or until the edges are slightly charred, then turn and roast for a further 10–15 minutes or until the chicken is slightly charred all over. Turn off the oven and leave the chicken inside with the door slightly ajar for 20–30 minutes.

Meanwhile, to make the relish, put all the ingredients in a small blender and process until smooth. Add a splash of water to give the relish a saucy consistency. Adjust the seasoning as needed.

Arrange the chicken on a warm platter and serve with the relish.

OVEN-BAKED TANDOORI CHICKEN WITH MINT AND CORIANDER RELISH

Butterflied roast chicken with chipotle lentil sauce

Serves 4

I love chicken cooked like this, but it's important that you don't overcook it, especially the breast. If the breast is perfect but the legs are still a little pink on the bone, remove the legs and finish cooking them in a frying pan – I promise you it's worth it to avoid eating stringy, dry breast. You can make the sauce from any tinned legumes. Serve the chicken with steamed greens drizzled with a great extra virgin olive oil, lemon juice, sea salt and lots of freshly ground black pepper. Boil some new potatoes until almost cooked, then roast them with the chook to pick up the lovely flavours.

2 kg (4 lb 8 oz) whole free-range chicken
sea salt and freshly ground black pepper
2 tablespoons extra virgin olive oil, plus extra to serve
1 lemon, cut into wedges
20 g (³/4 oz) thyme sprigs
a few flat-leaf (Italian) parsley sprigs

Chipotle lentil sauce

1 tablespoon extra virgin olive oil
1 small brown onion, finely diced
2 garlic cloves, chopped
sea salt
2 teaspoons chipotle chilli powder, or to taste
1 x 400 g (14 oz) tin brown lentils, rinsed and drained
130 g (4¹/2 oz/¹/2 cup) plain yoghurt

Take the chicken out of the fridge 2 hours before cooking.

Preheat the oven to 200°C (400°F) and line a large roasting tin with baking paper.

Put the chicken on a chopping board, cut off the neck and wing tips and remove the wishbone and parsons nose. Stand the chicken with the bottom facing up, and use a large sharp knife to cut down each side of the backbone and remove it. Press down on the chicken to butterfly it. Season the outside with sea salt and rub with the olive oil.

Scatter the lemon wedges and herbs over the base of the roasting tin and put the chicken on top, skin side up. Roast for 20 minutes, then reduce the oven temperature to 150°C (300°F) and cook for a further 35 minutes.

While the chicken is roasting, make the sauce. Heat the olive oil in a frying pan over medium–low heat. Add the onion, garlic and a good dose of sea salt, and gently cook, stirring from time to time, for about 20 minutes or until the onion is very tender. Add the chilli powder and cook for 1 minute, then stir in the lentils and cook until heated through. Stir in the yoghurt and remove from the heat. Blend the sauce with a stick blender until smooth; check the seasoning.

Remove the chicken from the oven, cover it with foil and two clean tea towels to keep warm, then set aside to rest for 15 minutes.

Place the chicken on a chopping board. Cut off the legs, then cut in half at the thigh and drumstick joint. Cut the breast in half down the middle, then cut each half into two pieces so that each piece has about the same amount of meat.

Squeeze the cooked lemon wedges into the beautiful chicken juices in the roasting tin and stir in a dash of extra virgin olive oil.

Put some of the lentil sauce on four large plates, then put a leg and breast piece on top. Spoon the pan juices over the chicken, add a good grind of black pepper and serve with the remaining lentil sauce in a bowl at the table.

Barbecued yakitori chicken

Serves 4

Make this a Japanese-inspired meal by serving the chicken with a bowl of rice and miso soup on the side. The chicken thighs can be replaced with any cut of chicken you like; wings would be fantastic. You could also use a mixture of pieces, such as breast, wings, livers and hearts – this is a terrific way to cook chicken offal. The yakitori sauce is great as a glaze over stir-fried chicken and vegetables.

8 boneless free-range chicken thighs, skin on
8 large, thick spring onions (scallions), trimmed
vegetable oil, for brushing
shichimi togarashi, to serve
lemon wedges, to serve

Yakitori sauce
60 ml (2 fl oz / $1/4$ cup) sake
50 ml ($1^{1}/_{2}$ fl oz) Japanese soy sauce
1 tablespoon mirin
3 teaspoons caster (superfine) sugar

Soak 8 wooden skewers in water for at least 2 hours.

To make the yakitori sauce, mix all the ingredients together in a small saucepan. Bring to the boil, then reduce the heat and simmer for 10 minutes or until the sauce has thickened to a glazing consistency.

Cut the chicken into 2–3 cm ($^{3}/_{4}$–$1^{1}/_{4}$ inch) pieces and cut the spring onions into 3 cm ($1^{1}/_{4}$ inch) lengths. Thread the chicken pieces and spring onions onto the skewers, using two pieces of chicken for each piece of spring onion.

Preheat a barbecue on high heat (I like these done over charcoal if possible). Brush the grill bars with vegetable oil. Grill the chicken for about 2 minutes on each side or until the juices drip (don't overcook the chicken). Remove the skewers from the grill and brush with the yakitori sauce. Return to the grill for 30 seconds on each side, then repeat the glazing and grilling process twice until the chicken is cooked through.

Place the skewers on serving plates, sprinkle with shichimi togarashi and serve with lemon wedges.

Note
Shichimi togarashi is a Japanese spice mix of between seven and nine different ingredients, such as chilli flakes, sansho pepper, dried citrus peel, sesame seeds, poppy seeds, hemp seeds, ginger, garlic, shiso and nori. Buy some and you will be sprinkling it on all your barbecued food. If you buy a small Japanese barbecue and get some charcoal, I promise you will be cooking 'stick food' all the time.

Korean spice-rubbed chicken

Serves 4

The chicken is great cut up and served with kimchi and gochujang (Korean hot bean paste), wrapped in lettuce leaves.

4 large boneless, skinless free-range
    chicken thighs
2 teaspoons light brown sugar
2 teaspoons gochugaru (Korean
    chilli powder)
1 teaspoon sea salt
1 teaspoon freshly ground black pepper
1/2 teaspoon sesame seeds
1 tablespoon sunflower oil

Marinade
60 ml (2 fl oz / 1/4 cup) sunflower oil
2 tablespoons soy sauce
1 tablespoon rice vinegar
2 garlic cloves, finely chopped

To make the marinade, whisk together the sunflower oil, soy sauce, rice vinegar and garlic in a large bowl.

Add the chicken to the marinade and set aside to marinate for at least 30 minutes.

Combine the brown sugar, gochugaru, sea salt, black pepper and sesame seeds in a small bowl. Drain the chicken well and pat dry with paper towel. Rub the dry spice mix evenly over the chicken.

Heat the sunflower oil on a barbecue or in a chargrill pan or frying pan over medium heat. Cook the chicken for about 4 minutes on each side, depending on the thickness, or until firm to the touch. Transfer to a plate and rest in a warm place for about 5 minutes.

Serve the chicken with any juices from the resting plate.

Note
Gochugaru is a Korean spice traditionally made by drying red chillies and crushing them into flakes. Usually the seeds are removed.

Chicken stir-fried in XO sauce

Serves 4 as part of a shared banquet

You can buy XO sauce these days, but it's really not that hard to make and yours will taste ten times better than one that comes out of a bottle. Make a big batch and keep it in the fridge to use in other dishes.

60 ml (2 fl oz/$^1/_4$ cup) vegetable oil

400 g (14 oz) boneless, skinless free-range chicken thighs, each cut into 3 pieces

1 large red capsicum (pepper), cut into large squares

200 g (7 oz) green beans, halved

4 spring onions (scallions), cut into 6 cm (2$^1/_2$ inch) lengths

1 tablespoon shaoxing rice wine

1 tablespoon light soy sauce, or to taste

30 g (1 oz) fresh black fungi, torn into bite-sized pieces

XO sauce

2 tablespoons dried shrimp, soaked in hot water for 2 hours

2$^1/_2$ tablespoons vegetable oil

4 long fresh red chillies, halved, seeded and roughly chopped

8 garlic cloves, finely chopped

1 small knob fresh ginger, peeled and finely chopped

$^1/_4$ teaspoon sea salt

$^1/_2$ teaspoon caster (superfine) sugar

1 tablespoon light soy sauce

1 tablespoon finely chopped spring onion (scallion)

To make the XO sauce, drain and roughly chop the shrimp. Heat the oil in a small frying pan over low heat. Sweat the chillies, garlic and ginger until soft. Add the shrimp and gently sauté for about 10 minutes. Add the sea salt and sugar and cook for a few moments, then add the soy sauce. Remove from the heat and stir in the spring onion.

Heat half the vegetable oil in a wok over high heat until very hot. Add the chicken pieces and stir-fry for about 5 minutes or until golden and just cooked. Remove the chicken from the wok and set aside.

Heat the remaining vegetable oil in the wok until smoking, add the capsicum and beans and stir-fry for 1 minute or until tender. Return the cooked chicken to the wok, then add the spring onions and shaoxing. Reduce the heat, add the XO sauce, soy sauce and black fungi and mix thoroughly. Check the seasoning, adding more soy sauce if needed.

Spoon the stir-fried chicken and vegetables onto a serving platter and serve immediately.

CHICKEN STIR-FRIED IN XO SAUCE

Grilled quail with harissa

Serves 4

Serve the quail with couscous or rice and your favourite salad leaves –
witlof (chicory) and radicchio with herbs or baby cos (romaine) or iceberg
lettuce is a nice combination. You can replace the quail with chicken:
simply grill four chicken breasts, being careful not to overcook and dry
them out. The harissa will keep well in the fridge: I find it addictive and
use it on barbecued and pan-fried meat and fish.

4 large quails, butterflied,
    backbones removed
mixed salad leaves and herbs, to serve
extra virgin olive oil, for drizzling
lemon wedges, to serve
sea salt and freshly ground black pepper

Marinade
2 tablespoons extra virgin olive oil
1 tablespoon finely chopped garlic
pinch of ground coriander
pinch of ground cumin
pinch of sweet paprika
pinch of sea salt

Harissa
1/4 teaspoon coriander seeds
1/4 teaspoon fennel seeds
1/2 teaspoon cumin seeds
2 tablespoons grapeseed oil
4 garlic cloves, thinly sliced
1 large red capsicum (pepper), diced
1 tablespoon finely chopped light palm
    sugar (jaggery)
2 teaspoons fish sauce
pinch of chilli powder

To make the marinade, combine the olive oil, garlic, spices and sea
salt in a small bowl and mix well.

Put the quails in a large shallow bowl, smother with the spiced oil and
marinate in the fridge for 1–2 hours. Remove the quails from the fridge
1 hour before cooking.

To make the harissa, toast the coriander, fennel and cumin seeds in a
dry frying pan until fragrant, watching to make sure they don't burn.
Transfer to a mortar and crush with a pestle or use a spice grinder to
grind until fine, then set aside.

Heat the grapeseed oil in a heavy-based frying pan over very low heat.
Add the garlic and capsicum and sweat for about 1 hour or until very
soft, stirring often to prevent sticking. Increase the heat, add the palm
sugar and cook for about 5 minutes or until well caramelised. The
mixture should turn a reddish brown. Stir in the fish sauce, reserved
toasted spices and chilli powder and cook for 2 minutes. Allow to
cool, then use a stick blender to blend until smooth.

Preheat a barbecue grill on medium–high heat. Place the quails on the
grill, skin side down, and cook for 3–4 minutes or until golden. Turn
and cook for another 3–4 minutes or until golden. Rest the quails for
5 minutes in a warm place.

Arrange some salad leaves and herbs on four serving plates. Dress
with extra virgin olive oil and a squeeze of lemon juice and season with
sea salt and black pepper. Put a quail on each plate and serve with a
dollop of harissa.

GRILLED QUAIL WITH HARISSA

Wok-fried duck with coconut milk, Thai basil and vermicelli

Serves 4

Anything with duck seems slightly decadent – probably why I love this dish. You can add or take away any number of items here to suit your palate. I like to add coriander (cilantro), long-leafed mint and fried garlic slivers and swap the vermicelli with thick fresh rice noodles. All are delicious! You can use chicken, squid, crab, prawns (shrimp) or sliced beef instead of duck.

600 g (1 lb 5 oz) boneless duck breasts,
    skin on
2 garlic cloves, thinly sliced
1 lemongrass stem, pale part only,
    thinly sliced
1 long fresh red chilli, thinly sliced on
    the diagonal
80 ml (2^1/$_2$ fl oz/^{1}/$_3$ cup) vegetable oil
1 large white onion, halved and
    thickly sliced
310 ml (10^3/$_4$ fl oz/1^1/$_4$ cups) coconut milk
2 tablespoons fish sauce
1 tablespoon oyster sauce
1 tablespoon tamarind paste
1 tablespoon caster (superfine) sugar
pinch of sea salt
20 g (^{3}/$_4$ oz/^{1}/$_4$ cup) crispy fried shallots
1 large handful Thai basil leaves
200 g (7 oz) dried rice vermicelli, cooked
    as per directions on packet, drained

Put the duck on a board, skin side down, and cut it into 5 mm (^{1}/$_4$ inch) slices, starting at the pointed end and following the natural angle of the meat so you end up with strips of even length.

Put the duck, garlic, lemongrass and chilli in a bowl and mix well.

Heat 60 ml (2 fl oz/^{1}/$_4$ cup) of the vegetable oil in a wok until smoking. Stir-fry the duck mixture in batches for 1–2 minutes or until golden and cooked through. Transfer the duck mixture to a plate and set aside.

Add the remaining oil to the wok and stir-fry the onion for 1–2 minutes or until light golden. Return the duck mixture to the wok, pour in the coconut milk and bring to the boil. Reduce the heat and simmer for 2 minutes. Season with the fish sauce, oyster sauce, tamarind paste, sugar and sea salt. Simmer for a few minutes more, then check the seasoning and adjust if needed.

Garnish the duck with the fried shallots and Thai basil leaves and serve immediately with the vermicelli.

WOK-FRIED DUCK WITH COCONUT MILK, THAI BASIL AND VERMICELLI

Duck, olive and date tagine

Serves 4

Buy duck Marylands – leg quarters that have both the thigh and drumstick. You can substitute the duck with chicken or even lamb – just adjust the cooking time to suit. A raw fennel salad, steamed couscous and a dollop of Harissa (page 150) are great accompaniments to this dish.

6 duck Marylands (leg quarters)
250 ml (9 fl oz/1 cup) Chermoula (page 66)
1 red onion, cut into 6 wedges
2 carrots, peeled and thickly sliced
1 orange sweet potato, peeled and cut into chunks
400 g (14 oz) green beans, trimmed
40 g (1^1/$_2$ oz/^{1}/$_4$ cup) blanched almonds
sea salt
1 tablespoon extra virgin olive oil
2 tablespoons honey
juice of 1 lemon
8 fresh dates, pitted
1 small handful large green olives, pitted
^{1}/$_4$ preserved lemon, pith removed and rind finely chopped
1 large handful coriander (cilantro) leaves, chopped
1 large handful flat-leaf (Italian) parsley leaves, chopped

Cut the duck legs in half at the thigh and drumstick joint. Combine the duck pieces with the chermoula, onion, carrots, sweet potato, beans, almonds and a little sea salt in a bowl. Leave to marinate for about 1 hour.

Heat the olive oil in a tagine or a large saucepan with a tight-fitting lid. Add the duck, vegetables and any marinade to the pan and arrange the duck and vegetables so they are reasonably flat. Half-cover with water, add the honey and lemon juice and cover with the lid. Bring to the boil, then reduce the heat to a very gentle simmer.

After about 30 minutes, remove the lid and carefully turn the duck and vegetables over. Add the dates and olives, cover and cook for a further 30 minutes or until the duck and vegetables are tender. Remove from the heat.

You can serve the duck in the tagine or pan you cooked it in, spoon it onto a large platter or divide it among individual plates (there are three duck pieces per person). Just before serving, sprinkle the tagine with the preserved lemon rind, coriander and parsley.

DUCK, OLIVE AND DATE TAGINE

Pork and veal are also meats that you want to always buy free-range and, if possible, organic. Check out where your food comes from; it's better for you in the long run. Oh yes, and don't overcook it or it'll be dry – a bit of rosy juice is okay.

Chargrilled marinated pork cutlets with green papaya salad

Serves 2

The cutlets are fabulous grilled but I also like to crumb and pan-fry them before topping them with the salad.

2 pork cutlets, about 250 g (9 oz) each
vegetable oil, for brushing

Marinade
2 lemongrass stems, pale part only, finely chopped
1–2 small fresh red chillies, chopped
1 tablespoon shaoxing rice wine
1 tablespoon fish sauce
1 tablespoon vegetable oil

Papaya salad dressing
60 ml (2 fl oz/¼ cup) fish sauce
1 tablespoon caster (superfine) sugar
juice of 2 lemons
1 small garlic clove, finely chopped
2 long fresh red chillies, finely chopped

Papaya salad
½ green papaya, peeled, seeded and julienned
1 large handful mint leaves
2 tablespoons crispy fried shallots
2 tablespoons roasted unsalted cashews, roughly chopped
2 spring onions (scallions), julienned

To make the marinade, mix the lemongrass, chilli, shaoxing, fish sauce and vegetable oil together in a shallow bowl.

Coat the pork cutlets in the marinade, cover with plastic wrap and marinate in the fridge for at least 30 minutes. Remove the cutlets from the fridge at least 30 minutes before cooking.

While the meat is marinating, make the dressing. Pour the fish sauce into a small bowl, add the sugar and stir until dissolved. Whisk in the remaining ingredients until combined.

Brush a hot chargrill pan with a little vegetable oil and cook the pork cutlets for about 4 minutes on each side, depending on the thickness (don't overcook them). Transfer to a plate, cover with foil and a couple of clean tea towels and rest for 10 minutes.

While the meat is resting, toss all the salad ingredients together in a bowl with the dressing.

Put the cutlets on a chopping board and remove the bones. Thinly slice the meat and arrange on a plate. Arrange the salad on top of the meat and serve immediately.

CHARGRILLED MARINATED PORK CUTLETS WITH GREEN PAPAYA SALAD

Crumbed pork with lemon

Serves 4

Cut the pork off the bone and put it in a crusty bread roll with some coleslaw for a special sandwich.

4 x 200 g (7 oz) French-trimmed
    pork cutlets
75 g (2^1/$_2$ oz/^{1}/$_2$ cup) plain
    (all-purpose) flour
sea salt and freshly ground black pepper
1 large free-range egg
60 ml (2 fl oz/^{1}/$_4$ cup) milk
90 g (3^1/$_4$ oz/1^1/$_2$ cups) Japanese panko
    breadcrumbs
2 teaspoons chopped thyme leaves
2 teaspoons chopped flat-leaf (Italian)
    parsley leaves
80 ml (2^1/$_2$ fl oz/^{1}/$_3$ cup) extra virgin olive
    oil, plus extra if needed
40 g (1^1/$_2$ oz) unsalted butter, plus extra
    if needed
lemon wedges, to serve

Lightly pound each pork cutlet with a mallet to flatten slightly.

Put the flour in a shallow bowl and season with sea salt and black pepper. Add the egg and milk to another shallow bowl and whisk together. Combine the breadcrumbs and chopped herbs in a third shallow bowl.

Coat each pork cutlet in the flour, then shake away the excess. Next, dip into the egg mixture, let the excess drip off and then coat evenly in the breadcrumb mixture. Place on a plate in a single layer.

Heat the olive oil and butter in a large heavy-based frying pan over medium heat. When the butter has melted, add the cutlets and cook for about 4 minutes on each side or until golden brown. Add more butter and oil if the pan starts to look a bit dry.

Serve the hot cutlets with the lemon wedges.

Italian pork and pea ragù

Serves 4

Ragù is delicious served on soft polenta, short pasta or perhaps some steamed rice. Braise it over low heat so the pork is meltingly tender – slow, controlled cooking is the secret to a tender braise.

1.5 kg (3 lb 5 oz) pork shoulder, cut into
    3 cm (1¼ inch) dice
60 ml (2 fl oz/¼ cup) olive oil, plus extra
    to serve
1 brown onion, finely chopped
2 garlic cloves, finely chopped
sea salt and freshly ground black pepper
2 tablespoons tomato paste
    (concentrated purée)
1 tablespoon plain (all-purpose) flour
500 ml (17 fl oz/2 cups) Fresh chicken
    stock (page 56)
200 ml (7 fl oz) tomato passata
140 g (5 oz/1 cup) frozen peas, blanched
    and refreshed
finely grated parmesan cheese, to serve

Marinade
1 brown onion, chopped
1 celery stalk, chopped
2 fresh bay leaves
6 juniper berries
6 black peppercorns
2 rosemary sprigs
500 ml (17 fl oz/2 cups) cabernet sauvignon

Mix all the marinade ingredients together in a large bowl. Add the pork to the marinade and refrigerate for about 8 hours.

Remove the pork from the marinade, drain and pat dry with paper towel. Strain the marinade through a fine sieve, reserving the liquid and discarding the solids.

Heat 2 tablespoons of the olive oil in a deep heavy-based frying pan with a tight-fitting lid. Seal the marinated pork in batches over high heat until golden brown on the outside, then remove from the pan and set aside.

Reduce the heat to low and add the remaining olive oil to the frying pan. Add the onion, garlic and sea salt and cook for about 10 minutes or until the onion is softened. Stir in the tomato paste and cook for a few minutes, then add the flour and cook, stirring, for about 3 minutes.

Gradually whisk in 400 ml (14 fl oz) of the reserved marinade. Bring to the boil, then reduce the heat and simmer for 5 minutes, whisking constantly to prevent lumps forming. Add the stock, passata, pork and its juices to the pan. There should be enough liquid to cover the pork. Place a sheet of baking paper directly on top of the liquid and bring to a simmer. Cover with a lid and cook for about 1 hour or until the pork is tender.

Discard the baking paper and transfer the pork to a bowl with a slotted spoon. Gently simmer the sauce for 10 minutes or until slightly thickened. Return the meat to the pan and add the peas. Check the seasoning and give a good grind of black pepper.

Serve the ragù with plenty of freshly grated parmesan and a splash of extra virgin olive oil.

ITALIAN PORK AND PEA RAGÙ

Roast pork belly with balsamic-marinated red onions

Serves 4

Marinating the onions takes away their harshness, and the combination of the sweet–savoury vinegar and the texture of the onion is perfect with the crisp pork. Make sure the oil is super-hot when you are spooning it over the pork skin – this is the key to crazy-crisp crackling.

The night before you cook the pork, use a clean utility knife or razor blade to score lines in the pork skin from the top to the bottom, about 3 mm (^{1}/$_8$ inch) apart. Cut through the skin but don't cut into the flesh. Using your fingers, rub the red wine vinegar into the pork skin. Next, using a massaging action, rub sea salt into the skin, then put the uncovered pork on a plate in the fridge to dry overnight.

Cut the onions into wedges and sprinkle with sea salt. After about 2 hours, wash away the salt, pat the onions dry, place in a bowl and cover with the balsamic vinegar. Cover and refrigerate overnight.

Remove the pork from the fridge about 3 hours before cooking.

Preheat the oven to 180°C (350°F). Put the pork on a wire rack in a roasting tin, skin side up, and roast, undisturbed, for 30 minutes. At this stage, check the pork's core temperature with a meat thermometer. If it has reached about 71°C (160°F), remove the pork from the oven; if not, return it to the oven and keep checking the core temperature. Turn the oven down or leave the door ajar so the temperature drops to around 60°C (140°F). Return the meat to the oven to rest for about 30 minutes. During this time the meat's core temperature should rise to around 75°C (167°F) – be sure to check it.

Just before serving, heat the vegetable oil in a small saucepan until it is just smoking. Remove the roasting tin from the oven and carefully spoon the hot oil over the pork skin to finish the crackling.

Cut the pork into strips (often it's easier to cut the crackling with a bread knife) and divide among four plates. Drain the onions and arrange beside the pork. Drizzle a little balsamic vinegar and olive oil over the meat, give a really good grind of black pepper and serve.

1 kg (2 lb 4 oz) pork belly
60 ml (2 fl oz / ^{1}/$_4$ cup) red wine vinegar
sea salt and freshly ground black pepper
3 small red onions
250 ml (9 fl oz / 1 cup) aged balsamic
    vinegar, plus extra to serve
500 ml (17 fl oz / 2 cups) vegetable oil
extra virgin olive oil, to serve

ROAST PORK BELLY WITH BALSAMIC-MARINATED RED ONIONS

Stir-fried pork with hot bean paste

Serves 4

I love this simple stir-fry. I like to use the sichuan hot bean paste called pixian, which is made from fermented broad beans rather than soy beans. It is super-complex and very salty, but totally addictive. I also like to make this recipe using gochujang (Korean hot bean paste) instead of the Chinese hot bean paste.

80 ml (2 1/2 fl oz / 1/3 cup) peanut oil
300 g (10 1/2 oz) pork fillet, thinly sliced
100 g (3 1/2 oz) snow peas (mangetout), trimmed
1 small knob fresh ginger, peeled and finely grated
8 garlic cloves, finely chopped
3 tablespoons Chinese hot bean paste
1 tablespoon shaoxing rice wine
1 tablespoon light soy sauce
1 tablespoon Chinese black vinegar
1 teaspoon sugar
60 ml (2 fl oz / 1/4 cup) Fresh chicken stock (page 56)
freshly ground white pepper
2 spring onions (scallions), thinly sliced
1 small handful coriander (cilantro) sprigs

Heat a wok until smoking, then add half the peanut oil. When the oil is hot, stir-fry the pork in batches until just coloured and almost cooked through. Transfer the pork to a plate and wipe the wok clean.

Reheat the wok with another 1 tablespoon of the peanut oil and stir-fry the snow peas until just tender; remove them from the wok also.

Heat the remaining peanut oil in the wok and stir-fry the ginger, garlic and hot bean paste until fragrant. Deglaze the wok with the shaoxing, then add the soy sauce, vinegar, sugar and stock and simmer for 2 minutes. Return the stir-fried pork and snow peas to the wok and toss together.

Spoon the pork mixture onto a serving plate or into bowls, add a good grind of white pepper and sprinkle with the spring onions and coriander to serve.

Braised veal

Serves 4

A tender veal braise goes beautifully with potato purée or soft polenta. Instead of an osso buco cut, I often use small bobby veal shanks that are cooked and served whole.

2 kg (4 lb 8 oz) veal osso buco, cut into 3 cm (1^1/$_4$ inch) slices
plain (all-purpose) flour, for dusting
60 ml (2 fl oz/^{1}/$_4$ cup) extra virgin olive oil
1 brown onion, finely chopped
3 carrots, peeled and finely chopped
4 celery stalks, finely chopped
sea salt and freshly ground black pepper
170 ml (5^1/$_2$ fl oz/^{2}/$_3$ cup) cabernet merlot
2 litres (70 fl oz/8 cups) Fresh chicken stock (page 56)
6 garlic cloves
4 bay leaves
4 thyme sprigs

Preheat the oven to 200°C (400°F).

Lightly coat the veal pieces with flour. Warm the olive oil in a flameproof casserole dish over medium–high heat. Add the veal pieces and sear until golden on all sides, then transfer to a plate.

Reduce the heat, add the onion, carrots and celery to the casserole dish with a pinch of sea salt and sauté for a few minutes or until the vegetables are starting to colour. Deglaze the casserole with the wine, scraping the base with a wooden spoon, then simmer for 1 minute.

Return the veal to the casserole and add the stock, garlic, bay leaves and thyme. Bring to a simmer, then place a sheet of baking paper directly on top of the liquid to help retain moisture during cooking. Cover with a lid and transfer to the oven. Bake for 3^1/$_2$ hours, turning the veal halfway through, or until the meat is beginning to fall off the bone. Remove from the oven, add a grind of black pepper and check the seasoning.

Put the veal pieces on four plates and spoon over the sauce to serve.

Pan-fried veal with mustard fruits and braised greens

Serves 4

Here the veal can be crumbed if you like, or you could use chicken instead. The braised greens work with just about anything. I probably eat them once a week with roasts and barbecues. Mustard fruits add a great crispy texture. They are available in gourmet food stores and specialist delicatessens.

700 g (1 lb 9 oz) piece veal fillet, cut into 8 medallions
sea salt and freshly ground black pepper
40 g (1^1/$_2$ oz) butter
1 tablespoon extra virgin olive oil
140 g (5 oz) mustard fruits, drained

Braised greens
300 g (10^1/$_2$ oz) cavolo nero
300 g (10^1/$_2$ oz) silverbeet (Swiss chard)
60 ml (2 fl oz/^{1}/$_4$ cup) extra virgin olive oil
1 small red onion, finely diced
2 garlic cloves, finely diced
2 anchovy fillets, finely diced
250 ml (9 fl oz/1 cup) Fresh chicken stock (page 56)
squeeze of lemon juice
sea salt and freshly ground black pepper

To prepare the greens, slice the cavolo nero and silverbeet leaves into 2 cm (^{3}/$_4$ inch) thick strips.

Heat the olive oil in a large saucepan over low heat. Add the onion, garlic and anchovies and cook, stirring, until the onion and garlic just start to colour. Add the stock, cavolo nero and silverbeet and stir to combine. Cover and simmer, stirring regularly, for about 25 minutes or until the leaves are very tender. They will lose their vibrancy and turn a deep green colour. Stir in the lemon juice and season to taste with sea salt and black pepper.

Meanwhile, season the veal with sea salt. Heat a large frying pan over medium–high heat. When hot, add the butter and olive oil. Cook the veal, turning once, for 2–3 minutes on each side or until golden. Remove the veal from the pan, season with black pepper and leave to rest in a warm place for 5 minutes.

While the veal is resting, cut the mustard fruits into bite-sized wedges.

Serve the veal on a plate of braised greens with a spoonful of mustard fruits on the side.

The best-tasting beef and lamb is grass-fed and, although it may at times be a little more firm than grain-fed meat, it's worth it. Prize flavour over everything else. Grass-fed meat is also better for the environment and high in omega-3 fatty acids.

Slow-roasted rack of lamb with quinoa salad and tahini sauce

Serves 4–6

These flavours work just as well with chicken too. When I roast garlic at home I always roast a bulb or two – I can never get enough of it, it's so addictive.

2 x 8-bone racks of lamb
sea salt and freshly ground black pepper
2 tablespoons extra virgin olive oil
20 g ($^3/_4$ oz) thyme sprigs
8 unpeeled garlic cloves
1 teaspoon ground sumac
135 g (4$^3/_4$ oz/$^1/_2$ cup) tahini
grated zest and juice of $^1/_2$ lemon

Quinoa salad

200 g (7 oz/1 cup) red or white quinoa
sea salt and freshly ground black pepper
grated zest and juice of $^1/_2$ lemon
80 ml (2$^1/_2$ fl oz/$^1/_3$ cup) extra virgin olive oil
100 g (3$^1/_2$ oz) pitted green olives, roughly chopped
100 g (3$^1/_2$ oz/$^2/_3$ cup) roasted pistachio nuts, roughly chopped
1 handful flat-leaf (Italian) parsley leaves, roughly chopped
1 handful mint leaves, roughly chopped

Preheat the oven to 90°C (195°F).

Trim off the fat from the lamb and season the meat with sea salt.

Heat 1 tablespoon of the olive oil in a frying pan over medium–high heat. Gently pan-fry the lamb racks until golden brown all over.

Make a bed of thyme and garlic in a roasting tin and put the lamb racks on top. Sprinkle the sumac over the lamb. Roast for 45–50 minutes or until a meat thermometer registers a core temperature of 54°C (129°F). Remove from the oven and allow the lamb to rest somewhere warm for 10 minutes. Check the garlic and return to the oven if needed to cook until very soft.

Meanwhile, to make the salad, add the quinoa to a saucepan with plenty of water and a pinch of sea salt. Bring to the boil, then reduce the heat and simmer, covered, for about 15 minutes or until tender. Drain off any remaining liquid and allow to cool. Dress the quinoa with the lemon zest, lemon juice, olive oil, sea salt and black pepper.

Squeeze the purée from two of the garlic cloves into a food processor and add the tahini, lemon zest, lemon juice, remaining olive oil, sea salt and black pepper. While the processor is running, add 125 ml (4 fl oz/$^1/_2$ cup) warm water in a steady stream. Stop and scrape down the side of the bowl, then continue to blend, adding enough water to give the sauce a dolloping consistency. Check the seasoning.

Just before serving, mix the quinoa with the olives, pistachios and herbs. Carve the lamb and serve it with the tahini sauce, quinoa salad and extra garlic cloves for those who love their roast garlic!

Note

Sumac is a dark crimson, almost purple spice that comes from the outer flesh of berries from a tree found in the Middle East.

SLOW-ROASTED RACK OF LAMB WITH QJINOA SALAD AND TAHINI SAUCE

Lamb shepherd's pies

Serves 4

Pot pies are really simple and this one is a classic. It can be topped with puff pastry if you find the potato too heavy. You can change the pie filling to beef – just cook it a little longer. Chicken is nice, too – change the red wine to white wine and reduce the cooking time. Serve the pie with a lovely tossed green salad.

1 kg (2 lb 4 oz) boneless lamb shoulder, cut into 4 cm (1^1/$_2$ inch) pieces
sea salt and freshly ground black pepper
2 tablespoons plain (all-purpose) flour
80 ml (2^1/$_2$ fl oz/^{1}/$_3$ cup) extra virgin olive oil, plus extra for drizzling
2 small brown onions, cut into 1 cm (^{1}/$_2$ inch) dice
2 large carrots, peeled and cut into 1 cm (^{1}/$_2$ inch) pieces
4 celery stalks, cut into 1 cm (^{1}/$_2$ inch) pieces
2 garlic cloves, finely chopped
2 teaspoons thyme leaves
1 tablespoon tomato paste (concentrated purée)
750 ml (26 fl oz/3 cups) full-bodied red wine
2 bay leaves
750 ml (26 fl oz/3 cups) Fresh chicken stock (page 56)

Mashed potato topping
800 g (1 lb 12 oz) all-purpose potatoes (e.g. desiree)
55 g (2 oz) butter
80 ml (2^1/$_2$ fl oz/^{1}/$_3$ cup) milk
80 ml (2^1/$_2$ fl oz/^{1}/$_3$ cup) thin (pouring) cream
pinch of sea salt
pinch of freshly cracked white pepper
40 g (1^1/$_2$ oz) parmesan cheese, grated

Preheat the oven to 130°C (250°F).

Season the lamb well with sea salt, then sprinkle with the flour, toss to coat lightly and shake away the excess. Pour half the olive oil into a large flameproof casserole dish or ovenproof pan with a tight-fitting lid and heat over high heat. Cook the lamb in batches until golden, transfer to a plate and set aside.

Reduce the heat, add the remaining olive oil to the pan and sauté the onions, carrots, celery, garlic and thyme for about 10 minutes or until the vegetables have softened and are starting to caramelise. Increase the heat slightly, stir in the tomato paste and cook for 2 minutes, then pour in the red wine and simmer until the liquid has reduced by about two-thirds. Return the lamb to the pan and add the bay leaves and stock. Bring to the boil, then cover and transfer the pan to the oven. Bake for 2^1/$_2$ hours or until the lamb is very tender.

Remove the pan from the oven and use a slotted spoon to transfer the lamb and vegetables to a bowl. Place the pan on the stove over high heat and simmer until the sauce has reduced to the consistency of a nice gravy. Fold the lamb and vegetables through the sauce. Check the seasoning and add a good grind of black pepper.

Increase the oven temperature to 160°C (315°F).

To make the potato topping, steam the whole potatoes until tender, then allow to cool slightly and slip off the skins. Mash the potatoes until smooth or push through a mouli.

Combine the butter, milk and cream in a saucepan, season with sea salt and white pepper and heat until almost boiling. Gradually add the hot liquid to the potatoes and mix to combine. Check the seasoning.

Divide the lamb mixture among four individual baking dishes or large ramekins and spoon the mashed potato on top. Sprinkle with the grated parmesan and drizzle with olive oil. Bake the pies for 10 minutes or until heated through. You can put them under the grill (broiler) to caramelise the cheese if needed. Serve warm with a nice salad.

Moussaka

Serves 4

Essentially a pasta-free lasagne, this lamb ragù with béchamel and eggplant is divine. There is a reason moussaka is one of the national dishes of Greece: it's just so darn good. You can make it in individual ramekins or ovenproof dishes if you prefer. These would be great for a dinner party or you could take the leftovers to work for lunch.

2 large eggplants (aubergines), cut into 5 mm ($1/4$ inch) slices

sea salt and freshly ground black pepper

2 tablespoons extra virgin olive oil, plus extra for brushing

2 small brown onions, finely chopped

4 garlic cloves, chopped

500 g (1 lb 2 oz) minced (ground) lamb

90 g ($3 1/4$ oz) tomato paste (concentrated purée)

1 x 400 g (14 oz) tin chopped tomatoes

$1/4$ teaspoon ground cinnamon or 1 cinnamon stick

1 teaspoon caster (superfine) sugar

1 large handful flat-leaf (Italian) parsley leaves, chopped

40 g ($1 1/2$ oz) grated parmesan cheese

Béchamel sauce

50 g ($1 3/4$ oz) butter

50 g ($1 3/4$ oz/$1/3$ cup) plain (all-purpose) flour

500 ml (17 fl oz/2 cups) milk, warmed

80 g ($2 3/4$ oz/$3/4$ cup) finely grated parmesan cheese

sea salt and freshly ground white pepper

Salt the eggplant slices on both sides and set aside for 1 hour. Rinse the eggplant under running water and then pat dry. Brush with a little olive oil and cook in a non-stick frying pan over medium–high heat for 2–3 minutes on each side or until golden. Remove from the pan and set aside. Wipe out the pan.

Heat the 2 tablespoons olive oil in the frying pan and sauté the onions over low heat for 4–5 minutes. Add the garlic and cook until the onions are soft. Add the lamb, increase the heat and stir-fry until browned. Season the lamb with salt, then add the tomato paste and cook for 2 minutes. Stir in the tomatoes, cinnamon and sugar. Bring to the boil, then reduce the heat, cover and simmer for about 20 minutes. Remove the lid and simmer for a few minutes more to thicken slightly if necessary. Check the seasoning and remove the cinnamon stick, if using. Fold the parsley through the sauce.

To make the béchamel sauce, melt the butter in a saucepan, add the flour and stir over low heat for 2–3 minutes or until the mixture is bubbling and grainy. Gradually pour in the warmed milk, stirring constantly, and cook until the mixture starts to boil and thicken. Stir in the parmesan and season to taste.

Preheat the oven to 180°C (350°F). Layer the braised lamb and fried eggplant two or three times in a large ovenproof dish, starting and finishing with a layer of eggplant if possible – the number of layers will depend on the size and depth of your dish. Spread the béchamel over the top and sprinkle liberally with the parmesan.

Bake for 25 minutes or until the moussaka has warmed through and the top is golden. Set aside for 5–10 minutes before serving.

Lamb with fennel, olives and preserved lemon

Serves 4

This simple braise is best served with couscous or rice. A nice date and orange salad would be a welcome addition. You can replace the lamb with chicken – just halve the cooking time and don't add as much water.

700 kg (1 lb 9 oz) boneless lamb shoulder, cut into 2.5 cm (1 inch) pieces
sea salt and freshly ground black pepper
60 ml (2 fl oz/¼ cup) extra virgin olive oil
2 red onions, sliced
4 garlic cloves, chopped
60 g (2¼ oz) preserved lemon rind, thinly sliced, plus extra to serve
1 teaspoon saffron threads, soaked in 2 tablespoons water
1 teaspoon ground ginger
1 teaspoon ground cumin
1 teaspoon chilli flakes
2 baby fennel bulbs, cut into wedges
175 g (6 oz/1 cup) green olives
1 handful flat-leaf (Italian) parsley leaves, roughly chopped

Season the lamb with sea salt. Heat the olive oil in a large heavy-based frying pan over high heat and fry the lamb in batches until golden brown. Transfer the lamb to a plate and set aside.

Add the onions and garlic to the pan and cook over medium heat until soft. Add the preserved lemon rind, saffron and water, ginger, cumin and chilli flakes and stir to combine.

Return the lamb to the pan with 500 ml (17 fl oz/2 cups) water and bring to the boil. Add the fennel and reduce the heat to a gentle simmer, then cover and cook for 30 minutes. Remove the lid and cook for a further 20 minutes or until everything is meltingly tender.

Remove the pan from the heat and stir in the olives and parsley. Spoon into four bowls, give a good grind of black pepper and serve.

Roast leg of lamb with skordalia

Serves 4–6

I recommend investing in a meat thermometer – it's worth its weight in gold, as it will deliver you a perfectly cooked roast every time. The higher the heat in the oven, the longer the meat will keep cooking. If you are taking the lamb straight from the fridge to the oven it will always take longer to cook. Skordalia is awesome with roasted or pan-fried chicken and fish as well.

2–3 kg (4 lb 8 oz–6 lb 12 oz) leg of lamb, shank on
extra virgin olive oil, for rubbing
sea salt and freshly ground black pepper
20 g (³/₄ oz) thyme sprigs

Skordalia
5 unpeeled garlic cloves
2 all-purpose potatoes (e.g. pink eye)
2 tablespoons almond meal
1 teaspoon sea salt
freshly ground black pepper
juice of 1 lemon
60 ml (2 fl oz / ¼ cup) extra virgin olive oil

Remove the lamb from the fridge 2 hours before cooking to let the meat come to room temperature.

Preheat the oven to 180°C (350°F). Place the lamb in a large roasting tin, rub with olive oil and season with plenty of sea salt and freshly ground black pepper. Lay the thyme over the lamb and place the whole garlic cloves for the skordalia in the tin. Roast the lamb for 20 minutes, then turn it over and turn the oven down to 160°C (315°F).

Continue cooking the lamb, turning it every 20 minutes. After 1 hour, start checking the meat's core temperature. The final resting temperature should be 60°C (140°F) and you need to factor in residual heat, so 55–56°C (131–133°F) should be fine. Once the lamb reaches that temperature, remove it from the oven and try to get the oven temperature down to 60°C (140°F), keeping the door ajar if necessary. Remove the garlic cloves and set aside for the skordalia. Once the oven has reached the right temperature, return the lamb to the oven to rest for 30 minutes.

While the lamb is resting, make the skordalia. Cook the whole potatoes in a pan of simmering salted water until tender. Drain and peel the potatoes, then pass through a potato ricer, coarse sieve or mouli and place in a bowl. Squeeze the roasted garlic flesh into the bowl and mix thoroughly. Add the almond meal, sea salt, black pepper and lemon juice and mix until incorporated. Add the olive oil in a thin stream, whisking all the time. Check the seasoning.

Place the lamb leg on a chopping board, positioning it on one of its sides. Holding the shank with a clean tea towel, take a sharp knife and, starting from the ball at the end of the bone, cut down the bone, removing one of the large muscles. Now turn the lamb around and remove the rest of the meat from the bone by cutting down each side of the bone and removing the large piece of muscle left. You should have two large pieces of meat on the board. Slice these pieces across the grain to give semi-circular slices. This will make the lamb more tender to eat.

Divide the lamb among serving plates and add a dollop of skordalia to each plate. Season and drizzle with the cooking juices to serve.

Braised beef cheeks with peas

Serves 4

A classic braise, lovely served with a potato purée. It's also good made with all chicken stock instead of veal and chicken; the finished dish will be a little lighter and not as sticky. Use a nice red wine – if you wouldn't drink it, why would you cook with it?

2 tablespoons extra virgin olive oil

1 kg (2 lb 4 oz) trimmed beef cheeks

3 garlic cloves, thinly sliced

2 brown onions, sliced

2 celery stalks, finely chopped

2 small carrots, finely chopped

2 teaspoons sea salt

375 ml (13 fl oz/1^1/$_2$ cups) full-bodied red wine

2 fresh bay leaves

3 thyme sprigs

250 ml (9 fl oz/1 cup) veal stock

500 ml (17 fl oz/2 cups) Fresh chicken stock (page 56)

freshly ground black pepper

75 g (2^1/$_2$ oz/^{1}/$_2$ cup) peas

Preheat the oven to 180°C (350°F).

Heat half the olive oil in a large flameproof casserole dish over medium–high heat. Add the beef cheeks and cook for 3–5 minutes on each side or until browned, then transfer to a plate.

Reduce the heat and add the remaining oil to the casserole dish, then add the garlic, onions, celery, carrots and sea salt. Cook for about 10 minutes or until the vegetables have softened. Pour in the wine and simmer for 5 minutes, then add the bay leaves, thyme, stocks and a grind of black pepper. Return the beef cheeks to the casserole dish and place a sheet of baking paper directly on top of the liquid, then bring to the boil.

Put the lid on the casserole dish and transfer to the oven. Cook for 3–3^1/$_2$ hours, turning halfway through, until the beef cheeks are very tender.

Use a slotted spoon to transfer the beef and vegetables to a plate. Place the casserole dish on the stove over medium heat and simmer until the sauce has reduced slightly. Return the beef and vegetables to the sauce, add the peas and cook until the peas are tender. Serve immediately with potato purée.

BRAISED BEEF CHEEKS WITH PEAS

Black pepper and chilli lamb

Serves 4 as part of a shared banquet

Instead of lamb, you could use sliced beef, pork or chicken. Sometimes I cook prawns (shrimp) this way, add some steamed greens and a bowl of rice and it's a fantastic meal.

1 teaspoon potato flour
1 tablespoon shaoxing rice wine
3 teaspoons soy sauce
250 g (9 oz) loin of lamb, thinly sliced
60 ml (2 fl oz/1/4 cup) Fresh chicken stock (page 56)
1 teaspoon oyster sauce
1 tablespoon cornflour (cornstarch), dissolved in 1 tablespoon water
60 ml (2 fl oz/1/4 cup) vegetable oil
1/2 small red onion, sliced
1 long fresh red chilli, sliced
1 long fresh green chilli, sliced
2 garlic cloves, chopped
1 teaspoon whole black peppercorns, toasted and crushed
1 large handful coriander (cilantro) sprigs

Mix the potato flour, shaoxing and 1 teaspoon of the soy sauce in a bowl. Add the lamb and toss to coat, then marinate for 20 minutes.

Combine the remaining soy sauce, chicken stock, oyster sauce and cornflour mixture in a small bowl and set aside.

Heat a wok until smoking, then add half the vegetable oil and stir-fry the lamb slices for 2–3 minutes or until browned. Remove the lamb from the wok and set aside.

Heat the remaining oil in the wok and stir-fry the onion, chillies, garlic and crushed black pepper until fragrant.

Return the lamb to the wok with the soy sauce mixture and stir-fry for a few minutes more. Spoon onto a large platter and sprinkle with the coriander to serve.

BLACK PEPPER AND CHILLI LAMB

Barbecued T-bone with red capsicum and lemon salsa

Serves 4

If you can get dry-aged beef you will turn a good meal into a great one – it's all about the quality of the beef here.

4 x 400–500 g (14 oz–1 lb 2 oz)
   T-bone steaks
sea salt
extra virgin olive oil, for rubbing
1 teaspoon toasted coriander seeds,
   lightly crushed

Red capsicum and lemon salsa

2 red capsicums (peppers)
1 teaspoon salted baby capers, rinsed
   well and drained
1 large handful flat-leaf (Italian) parsley
   leaves, finely chopped
1 lemon, segmented and finely chopped,
   plus juice of 1 lemon
100 ml (3 1/2 fl oz) extra virgin olive oil
sea salt and freshly ground black pepper

Remove the steaks from the fridge 2 hours before you intend to start cooking and season liberally with sea salt.

To make the salsa, barbecue the capsicums until blackened all over, place in a bowl and cover with plastic wrap. When cool enough to handle, peel or scrape off the blackened skin. Finely dice the capsicums, then add to a bowl with the remaining salsa ingredients. Mix well and set aside at room temperature.

Preheat a barbecue on high heat. Rub the steaks with olive oil and put them on the barbecue grill at a 45-degree angle to the bars. Halfway through cooking, turn the steaks 45 degrees. When done, turn them over and cook the same way on the other side. Cook the steaks until done to your liking. Put the steaks on a plate, loosely cover with foil and leave to rest near the warm barbecue for 10 minutes.

Place a steak on each serving plate and spoon the salsa over the top, then sprinkle with the crushed coriander seeds and serve immediately.

BARBECUED T-BONE WITH RED CAPSICUM AND LEMON SALSA

Meatball tagine with tomato sauce and eggs

Serves 4

This is great served with crusty bread, couscous, rice or steamed potatoes. The beef can be substituted with lamb or even chicken – just don't overcook it. This sauce is also lovely for poaching seafood.

500 g (1 lb 2 oz) minced (ground) beef
1 brown onion, grated
sea salt
185 ml (6 fl oz/$3/4$ cup) olive oil
50 g ($1 3/4$ oz/1 small bunch)
    coriander (cilantro), finely
    chopped (including stems)
3 garlic cloves, chopped
1 tablespoon smoked paprika
1 tablespoon ground cumin
1 tablespoon ground coriander
1 tablespoon ground fennel
2 teaspoons freshly ground black pepper
1 x 400 g (14 oz) tin chopped Italian
    tomatoes
4 free-range eggs
crusty bread, to serve

Combine the beef and onion in a large bowl and season with sea salt. Cover with plastic wrap and refrigerate overnight.

Wet your hands slightly to help prevent sticking, then roll the beef into 2 cm ($3/4$ inch) balls.

Heat a large deep frying pan over high heat and add the olive oil. When it is hot but not smoking, add the meatballs and brown them all over, then transfer to a plate.

Reduce the heat, add the chopped coriander, garlic and ground spices to the pan and cook for a few minutes. Stir in the tomatoes and gently simmer for 10 minutes. Add the meatballs and simmer for a further 5 minutes, shaking the pan from time to time. Check the seasoning.

Crack the eggs into the pan and simmer for 5 minutes or until the whites have just set (the yolks should still be soft). Immediately take the pan to the table and serve with crusty bread.

Bibimbap with beef and onions

Serves 4

Bibimbap is a classic Korean dish of rice topped with meat and pickled vegetables, a simple one-bowl dish that is so delicious and satisfying. You could get away without making the pickles, but they are very easy and add a slight sharpness to the dish that is very desirable.

300 g (10 1/2 oz) fillet steak, cut into thin strips
1 brown onion, halved and thinly sliced
60 ml (2 fl oz/1/4 cup) soy sauce
1 tablespoon gochujang (Korean hot bean paste), plus extra to serve
2 garlic cloves, chopped
1 tablespoon light brown sugar
2 teaspoons sesame oil
sea salt and freshly ground black pepper
400 g (14 oz/2 cups) jasmine rice, rinsed
1 tablespoon vegetable oil
2 handfuls baby English spinach
1 tablespoon toasted sesame seeds

Pickled cucumber and carrot
1 Lebanese (short) cucumber, peeled and sliced into thin strips
1 small carrot, cut into fine matchsticks
1 tablespoon sea salt
1 tablespoon caster (superfine) sugar
2 tablespoons rice vinegar

To make the pickled cucumber and carrot, toss the vegetables with the salt and set aside for 30 minutes. Dissolve the caster sugar in the rice vinegar. Drain and rinse the vegetables, then squeeze dry and toss with the sweet vinegar. Leave until ready to serve, then drain the vinegar from the vegetables.

Combine the beef, onion, soy sauce, gochujang, garlic, brown sugar, sesame oil and a pinch of sea salt and black pepper in a bowl. Set aside to marinate for 30 minutes.

Combine the rice and 700 ml (24 fl oz) water in a large saucepan and bring to the boil. Cover tightly, reduce the heat to very low and cook for 15 minutes or until the rice is just tender. Remove from the heat and rest for 5 minutes, then fluff with a fork.

Heat a wok over high heat, add the vegetable oil and stir-fry the marinated beef for 2–3 minutes or until nicely coloured and just cooked through. Add the spinach and stir-fry until just wilted.

Spoon the rice into four deep bowls, top with the beef mixture and some of the pickles and sprinkle with the sesame seeds and extra gochujang. Serve immediately.

Steak pizza-style

Serves 4

Crumbed veal also works well with this tomato sauce. You can just sauté escalopes of veal, but crumbing gives them a really nice texture. If you do use crumbed veal, some anchovies and a poached egg on top of each serve is pretty wicked.

4 x 200 g (7 oz) fillet steaks
sea salt and freshly ground black pepper
2 tablespoons extra virgin olive oil
4 garlic cloves, chopped
$1/4$ teaspoon mild chilli flakes
3 oregano sprigs, leaves chopped
250 ml (9 fl oz/1 cup) white wine
250 ml (9 fl oz/1 cup) tomato passata
1 handful flat-leaf (Italian) parsley leaves,
  roughly chopped

Cut the steaks in half horizontally, place each piece between two sheets of baking paper and flatten with a rolling pin until they are about 5 mm ($1/4$ inch) thick, minute-steak style. Season the steaks on both sides with sea salt.

Heat the olive oil in a large frying pan over medium heat until hot but not smoking. Add the steaks and cook quickly until browned – just 1 minute or less on each side. Transfer the steaks to a plate.

Reduce the heat slightly, add the garlic to the pan and briefly sauté. Add the chilli flakes, oregano and wine and cook, scraping the base of the pan, for about 4–5 minutes or until the liquid has reduced. Stir in the tomato passata and cook for 1 minute to reduce further, then return the steaks to the pan. Simmer for 3–5 minutes, turning the steaks halfway through.

Put the steaks in a serving dish, pour the sauce over the top and garnish with the parsley and a good grind of black pepper.

STEAK PIZZA-STYLE

Simple ma po tofu

Serves 4 as part of a shared banquet

A classic dish, this is a very simple recipe and yet it's so tasty. Here I've used silken tofu and it does give a great texture, almost like a delicate custard, but by all means use firm tofu if that's all you can find. It won't be quite as delicate, but the dish will be just as tasty. You could also serve this as a complete meal for two people, with some steamed rice alongside.

2 tablespoons vegetable oil
250 g (9 oz) minced (ground) beef
1 garlic clove, finely chopped
2 spring onions (scallions), thinly sliced on the diagonal, plus extra to serve
2 tablespoons Chinese hot bean paste
125 ml (4 fl oz/^{1}/$_2$ cup) Fresh chicken stock (page 56)
1 teaspoon shaoxing rice wine
1 teaspoon light soy sauce
^{1}/$_2$ teaspoon dark soy sauce
^{1}/$_2$ teaspoon chilli flakes
2 teaspoons caster (superfine) sugar
^{1}/$_4$ teaspoon sea salt
300 g (10^1/$_2$ oz) silken tofu, cut into 2 cm (^{3}/$_4$ inch) cubes
a good pinch of sichuan pepper
^{1}/$_2$ teaspoon sesame oil

Heat a wok until smoking, then add the vegetable oil and stir-fry the beef, garlic, spring onions and hot bean paste for 3 minutes or until the beef has browned and the ingredients are fragrant.

Add the chicken stock, shaoxing, soy sauces, chilli flakes, sugar and sea salt and bring to the boil, then reduce the heat and simmer for 2 minutes. Gently fold in the tofu, then bring back to a simmer and turn off the heat.

Add the sichuan pepper and sesame oil and gently mix together. Serve immediately, sprinkled with the extra spring onions.

Cinnamon and chilli braised beef

Serves 4 as part of a shared banquet

Tasty spiced beef goes well with egg noodles or rice. It's so easy to cook – it just needs time to braise until it's beautifully tender.

450 g (1 lb) beef brisket, cut into 4 cm (1^1/$_2$ inch) pieces
2 tablespoons peanut oil
2 small garlic cloves, finely chopped
1 small knob fresh ginger, peeled and finely chopped
60 ml (2 fl oz/^{1}/$_4$ cup) chilli bean sauce
1 tablespoon gochujang (Korean hot bean paste)
750 ml (26 fl oz/3 cups) Fresh chicken stock (page 56)
1 cinnamon stick
1 star anise
1 tablespoon light soy sauce
2 teaspoons caster (superfine) sugar
1 spring onion (scallion), thinly sliced

Put the beef pieces in a large saucepan of water and bring to the boil. When scum rises to the top, drain the beef, then rinse under running water and pat dry with paper towel.

Heat half the peanut oil in a wok with a lid over high heat. When the oil is smoking, add the beef pieces and sauté until well browned, then transfer to a plate.

Add the remaining oil to the wok and stir-fry the garlic and ginger until fragrant, then add the chilli bean sauce and gochujang and stir-fry for a few minutes more. Return the beef to the wok and add the stock and whole spices. Reduce the heat, cover and simmer over very low heat for about 1^1/$_2$ hours.

Remove the lid and cook for about 10 minutes or until the beef is tender and the liquid has reduced to a saucy consistency.

Stir in the soy sauce and sugar and check the seasoning. Serve sprinkled with the spring onion.

CINNAMON AND CHILLI BRAISED BEEF

If you're lucky enough to have a farmers' market nearby, you'll be getting the freshest veg – picked late the day before or even that same morning in some cases. Get behind the 'ugly veg' campaign that some stores are running – we currently plough a third of vegetables back into the ground because they don't meet buyers' specifications, yet they're just as delicious. Let's all do our bit to save the planet.

Braised witlof and leek gratin with gruyère

Serves 4 as a side dish

A truly wonderful dish. I think it's the slight bitterness of the witlof that really elevates it. Of course you can make it without the bacon, but the complexity of taste it brings means it's a great shame to leave it out.

4 heads witlof (chicory)

1 leek

20 g ($^3/_4$ oz) unsalted butter

1 tablespoon extra virgin olive oil

4 rindless back bacon rashers, finely diced

2 French shallots, finely chopped

2 garlic cloves, finely chopped

1 teaspoon sea salt

2 teaspoons thyme leaves, chopped

170 ml (5$^1/_2$ fl oz/$^2/_3$ cup) dry white wine

625 ml (21$^1/_2$ fl oz/2$^1/_2$ cups) Fresh chicken stock (page 56)

1$^1/_2$ tablespoons dijon mustard

1 fresh bay leaf

freshly ground white pepper

125 ml (4 fl oz/$^1/_2$ cup) thin (pouring) cream

100 g (3$^1/_2$ oz/1$^1/_4$ cups) finely grated gruyère cheese

30 g (1 oz/$^1/_2$ cup) Japanese panko breadcrumbs

Remove any damaged leaves from the witlof, then cut them in half lengthways. Trim the leek, removing the tough outer leaves and ends and using only the white and light green parts. Split the leek lengthways, then cut it in half crossways so the pieces are about the same length as the witlof.

Melt the butter with the olive oil in a large frying pan over medium heat. Add the witlof and leek and cook for about 7 minutes or until starting to brown. Transfer the vegetables to a plate.

Add the bacon, shallots, garlic, sea salt and half the thyme to the pan. Cook, stirring, for 3–4 minutes or until the bacon begins to crisp. Deglaze the pan with the wine, then add the stock, mustard, bay leaf and white pepper. Return the witlof and leek to the pan and bring to the boil, then reduce the heat and gently simmer for 8–10 minutes or until the witlof and leek are cooked but still firm.

Meanwhile, preheat the grill (broiler) to medium heat.

Transfer the vegetables to a shallow gratin dish. Increase the heat under the pan to high, pour in the cream and simmer for a few minutes to reduce and thicken slightly. Pour the sauce over the vegetables.

Mix the gruyère, breadcrumbs and remaining thyme together and sprinkle over the vegetables. Cook under the grill for 3–5 minutes or until golden brown, then serve immediately.

BRAISED WITLOF AND LEEK GRATIN WITH GRUYÈRE

Roast brussels sprouts with hazelnuts

Serves 6 as a side dish

Sprouts are the star of this dish, but it also works really well with zucchini (courgettes) or green beans or, in fact, a combination of all three.

50 g (1 3/4 oz / 1/3 cup) hazelnuts
450 g (1 lb) brussels sprouts,
    halved lengthways
60 ml (2 fl oz / 1/4 cup) extra virgin olive oil
sea salt and freshly ground black pepper
1 tablespoon lemon juice
2 teaspoons dijon mustard
1/2 red onion, very finely diced

Preheat the oven to 180°C (350°F). Spread the hazelnuts on a baking tray and roast for about 8 minutes or until golden. Tip onto a clean tea towel and rub with the towel to remove the papery skins. Roughly chop the hazelnuts and set aside.

Remove any discoloured outer leaves from the sprouts. Toss the sprouts with 1 tablespoon of the olive oil, some sea salt and black pepper in a bowl. Tip onto a baking tray and roast, shaking the tray from time to time, for 20–30 minutes or until the sprouts are softened in the centre and the edges are turning crispy brown.

Whisk the remaining olive oil with the lemon juice, mustard and onion and season to taste with salt and pepper.

If serving straight away, toss the dressing with the sprouts and hazelnuts in a bowl and serve warm. Alternatively, you can toss them together and gently warm in a large saucepan over low heat just before serving.

Cauliflower gratin

Serves 4–6 as a side dish

Cauliflower is one of my favourite vegetables. Because it's so big in flavour, it makes a great partner for just about anything, whether seafood, meat or poultry. Try making a simple cauliflower purée for an awesome sauce or soup: gently cook cauliflower florets until tender in just enough stock or milk to cover them, then purée the whole lot until smooth and season with salt and freshly ground white pepper. You can then push it through a fine sieve for a lovely silky texture.

600 ml (21 fl oz) thick (double) cream
$^1/_2$ teaspoon finely grated fresh nutmeg
sea salt and freshly ground black pepper
1 cauliflower, about 1.5 kg (3 lb 5 oz)
50 g (1$^3/_4$ oz/$^1/_2$ cup) grated
    cheddar cheese
25 g (1 oz/$^1/_4$ cup) grated
    parmesan cheese

Preheat the oven to 180°C (350°F).

Combine the cream and nutmeg in a saucepan over medium heat. Bring to the boil, then reduce the heat and simmer until reduced by half. Remove from the heat and season to taste with sea salt and black pepper.

Trim the cauliflower and separate it into florets. Place in an ovenproof dish in a single layer and pour the hot cream over the top. Sprinkle with the combined cheeses and bake for 20–30 minutes or until golden (if your oven has a top element, turn it on for the last few minutes to help the cheeses brown nicely). Set aside to cool slightly before serving.

Raspberry and yoghurt mousse cake

Serves 10–12

You can buy raspberry purée or you can make your own. Simply sprinkle fresh or frozen raspberries with enough caster or icing (confectioners') sugar to balance the tartness, allow them to macerate, then purée in a blender or food processor and pass through a sieve to remove the seeds.

220 g (7³/4 oz) wholemeal biscuits (granita biscuits or graham crackers), crushed
100 g (3¹/2 oz) unsalted butter, melted
fresh raspberries, to serve

Raspberry layer
3 titanium-strength gelatine sheets
500 g (1 lb 2 oz) raspberry purée
2 tablespoons caster (superfine) sugar
300 ml (10¹/2 fl oz) thin (pouring) cream, whipped to soft peaks

Yoghurt layer
3 titanium-strength gelatine sheets
300 ml (10¹/2 fl oz) thin (pouring) cream
240 g (8¹/2 oz) Greek-style yoghurt
75 g (2¹/2 oz/¹/3 cup) caster (superfine) sugar
1 teaspoon vanilla bean paste

Line the base and side of a 20 cm (8 inch) round spring-form cake tin with a double layer of plastic wrap, ensuring you have some excess hanging over the edge for easy removal.

Combine the biscuit crumbs with the melted butter in a bowl and mix well. Press the mixture evenly over the base of the tin. Refrigerate for about 30 minutes or until firm.

To make the raspberry layer, soften the gelatine sheets in cold water for 5 minutes. Warm 100 g (3¹/2 oz) of the raspberry purée with the sugar in a saucepan over low heat, stirring to dissolve the sugar. Gently squeeze the excess water from the gelatine sheets, then stir through the warm raspberry purée until dissolved. Whisk in the remaining raspberry purée and cool to room temperature, but do not allow the mixture to set.

Fold the whipped cream through the raspberry purée, spoon into the cake tin over the biscuit base and smooth the top. Refrigerate for about 1 hour or until set.

To make the yoghurt layer, soften the gelatine sheets in cold water for 5 minutes. Warm 60 ml (2 fl oz/¹/4 cup) of the cream in a saucepan over low heat. Gently squeeze the excess water from the gelatine sheets, then stir through the warm cream until dissolved. Cool slightly, then fold through the yoghurt.

Whip the remaining cream, sugar and vanilla bean paste until soft peaks form, then fold into the yoghurt mixture. Spoon the yoghurt mixture on top of the raspberry layer and smooth the top with a spatula. Return to the fridge for about 1 hour or until the yoghurt layer has set.

Remove the cake from the fridge and use a hot, clean knife to cut it into 10 or 12 pieces. Serve with fresh raspberries.

Note
Gelatine comes in a number of different types and graded strengths. Leaf gelatine is used in most professional kitchens because it sets clearer and with a smoother consistency than powdered gelatine. Titanium is the strongest type of leaf gelatine and helps to counteract the acidity of the fruit in this recipe; one leaf is approximately equivalent to 1¹/2 to 2 teaspoons of powdered gelatine.

RASPBERRY AND YOGHURT MOUSSE CAKE

Spiced date cake with crème anglaise

Serves 8–12

Crème anglaise is great with cakes, puddings and tarts. Once you've tried making it, you'll realise how simple it is. I quite like it poured over a plate of beautiful seasonal fruit. The cake is also delicious with whipped cream or a scoop of ice cream.

380 g (13 1/2 oz) pitted medjool dates, chopped
1/4 teaspoon bicarbonate of soda (baking soda)
300 ml (10 1/2 fl oz) boiling water
90 g (3 1/4 oz) unsalted butter, chopped and softened
185 g (6 1/2 oz/1 cup) light brown sugar
3 free-range eggs
225 g (8 oz/1 1/2 cups) self-raising flour
1/4 teaspoon ground cinnamon
pinch of ground cloves
pinch of ground ginger

Crème anglaise
600 ml (21 fl oz) milk
1/2 vanilla bean, split lengthways
7 free-range egg yolks
100 g (3 1/2 oz) caster (superfine) sugar

Preheat the oven to 180°C (350°F). Grease a deep 24 cm (9 1/2 inch) round cake tin and line the base and side with baking paper.

Put the dates in a heatproof bowl, add the bicarbonate of soda and boiling water and mix to combine. Allow to stand for 5 minutes, then blend or process until smooth.

Use an electric mixer to beat the butter and brown sugar in a small bowl until pale and creamy, then beat in the eggs, one at a time. Transfer the mixture to a larger bowl, sift the flour and spices over the top and gently fold into the butter mixture using a large metal spoon. Fold in the dates until well combined.

Pour the mixture into the prepared tin and bake for about 50 minutes or until cooked when tested with a skewer. Cover the top with foil during baking if overbrowning. Stand the cake in the tin for 10 minutes before turning onto a wire rack lined with baking paper to cool.

To make the crème anglaise, pour the milk into a saucepan, scrape in the vanilla seeds and add the vanilla bean. Bring the milk to scalding point (just below simmering), then remove from the heat and discard the vanilla bean.

Whisk the egg yolks and caster sugar together until creamy. Continue whisking while you pour the warm milk over the egg yolk mixture. Pour the mixture back into the saucepan and place over very low heat. Stir continuously using a heatproof spatula until the mixture thickens and coats the back of the spatula or until it reaches 82°C (180°F) on a thermometer. Do not boil the mixture or it will split. Pass the mixture through a sieve into a bowl sitting in iced water and stir to cool. Cover the crème anglaise with plastic wrap and chill before serving.

Serve the cake warm or at room temperature with the crème anglaise on the side.

SPICED DATE CAKE WITH CREME ANGLAISE

Berry, Sauternes and mascarpone trifle

Serves 8–10

Any fruit in season can be substituted for the berries. I would also spend some dollars on the wine – the better the wine tastes, the better the dessert. This is also wonderful with just whipped cream, natural vanilla extract and icing (confectioners') sugar added in place of the mascarpone.

185 g (6^1/$_2$ oz / 1^1/$_2$ cups) fresh raspberries
375 g (13 oz / 2^1/$_2$ cups) strawberries, hulled and quartered
375 g (13 oz) savoiardi (lady fingers)
525 ml (18 fl oz) Sauternes
75 g (2^1/$_2$ oz) dark chocolate

Mascarpone cream
3 free-range egg yolks plus 4 free-range egg whites
120 g (4^1/$_4$ oz) caster (superfine) sugar
375 g (13 oz) mascarpone cheese
150 ml (5 fl oz) thin (pouring) cream

To make the mascarpone cream, use an electric mixer with a whisk attachment to whisk the egg yolks and half the sugar together until light and pale. Add the mascarpone and mix on low speed until just combined. Whip the cream until soft peaks form, then fold through the mascarpone mixture.

Put the egg whites in a clean bowl and beat until foamy. Add the remaining sugar and beat until soft peaks form, then gently fold into the mascarpone mixture.

Spoon half the mascarpone cream into a 3 litre (105 fl oz) trifle bowl. Mix the berries together and scatter over the mascarpone cream. Dip the savoiardi into the Sauternes, then arrange on top of the berries. Spoon the remaining mascarpone cream over the top, cover and refrigerate for several hours.

Finely grate the chocolate over the trifle to serve.

BERRY, SAUTERNES AND MASCARPONE TRIFLE

Italian cheesecake

Serves 6–8

Here is a very simple ricotta cheesecake that you can liven up by adding some chopped candied fruit to the filling.

375 g (13 oz/2 1/2 cups) plain (all-purpose) or cake flour, plus extra for rolling
50 g (1 3/4 oz) caster (superfine) sugar
pinch of salt
150 g (5 1/2 oz) chilled unsalted butter, chopped, plus extra for greasing
2 large free-range eggs
2 tablespoons milk
icing (confectioners') sugar, for dusting

Filling
250 g (9 oz) cream cheese, softened
90 g (3 1/4 oz) caster (superfine) sugar
3 large free-range eggs
250 ml (9 fl oz/1 cup) thin (pouring) cream
750 g (1 lb 10 oz) drained fresh whole-milk ricotta
2 teaspoons natural vanilla extract
60 ml (2 fl oz/1/4 cup) rum
finely grated zest of 1 orange
finely grated zest of 1 lemon

Place the flour, sugar and salt in a food processor and pulse to combine. Add the butter and pulse until the mixture forms crumbs. Whisk together the egg and milk, add to the food processor and pulse until the dough just comes together. Gather two-thirds of the dough into a ball and gather the remaining dough into a separate ball. Wrap each ball in plastic wrap and refrigerate for at least 1 hour or overnight.

Preheat the oven to 160°C (315°F). Grease a 20 cm (8 inch) round spring-form cake tin with butter and line the base and side with baking paper. Wrap foil around the base and up the outside of the tin to catch any leaks during baking.

Lightly sprinkle your work surface with flour and roll the larger ball of dough into a 32 cm (12 1/2 inch) disc, about 3 mm (1/8 inch) thick, to fit the base and side of the prepared tin. Gently roll the dough around the rolling pin, place it over the tin and unroll loosely. Press the dough gently into the base and against the side. Trim off the excess with a knife. Refrigerate the pastry base until needed. Roll the remaining dough to the same thickness and cut it into 1 cm (1/2 inch) wide strips (use a pastry wheel if you have one). Place the strips on a tray lined with baking paper and refrigerate with the pastry base.

To make the filling, use an electric mixer to beat the cream cheese and sugar until smooth, then incorporate the eggs, one at a time. Gradually add the cream, then use a large metal spoon to fold in the ricotta, vanilla extract, rum and citrus zest. The mixture does not need to be smooth – it's nice to have some lumps of ricotta.

Spoon the ricotta mixture into the pastry base, then arrange the pastry strips over the top in a crisscross pattern and trim the edges as necessary. Bake the cheesecake for 45–55 minutes or until the filling has just set and the pastry is golden. Loosen the side of the tin and allow the cheesecake to cool to room temperature in the tin. Dust with icing sugar to serve.

Note
If you are making the cheesecake ahead of time, transfer it to the fridge once it has cooled. About 30 minutes before serving, remove the cheesecake from the fridge, then dust it with the icing sugar just before serving.

Summer fruit with Sauternes cream

Serves 8–10

This simple dessert is perfect served around Christmas time in Australia. We are blessed with an abundance of summer fruit, sweet and delicious, and this always makes for a light end to a great meal with family and friends.

300 g (10^1/$_2$ oz) fresh cherries, pitted
125 g (4^1/$_2$ oz/1 cup) fresh raspberries
2 white peaches, peeled and cut
    into wedges
2 white nectarines, peeled and cut
    into wedges
1 mango, peeled and sliced
50 g (1^3/$_4$ oz) caster (superfine) sugar

Sauternes cream
120 ml (4 fl oz) Sauternes or other
    dessert wine
30 ml (1 fl oz) orange juice
strips of zest from 1 orange, no white pith
100 g (3^1/$_2$ oz) caster (superfine) sugar
300 ml (10^1/$_2$ fl oz) thick (double) cream

Combine all the fruit in a large bowl, sprinkle with the sugar and macerate for 1 hour.

Meanwhile, to make the Sauternes cream, combine the wine, orange juice and orange zest in a bowl and set aside to infuse for 1 hour. Discard the orange zest, then add the sugar and stir until dissolved. Add the cream and whisk to soft peaks.

Divide the fruit among some nice glasses, then spoon the Sauternes cream over the top and serve.

Chocolate hazelnut tart with crème anglaise

Serves 8–12

This decadent tart also rocks with rich vanilla ice cream. Once you have perfected the tart case, you will realise it's quite straightforward to make, although you can use a ready-made one if you're short on time. You could use mini tart shells instead of the large one.

185 g (6 1/2 oz/1 1/4 cups) plain (all-purpose) flour, plus extra for dusting
100 g (3 1/2 oz) chilled unsalted butter, cubed, plus extra for greasing
1 1/2 tablespoons caster (superfine) sugar
1 teaspoon natural vanilla extract
1 free-range egg, lightly whisked
1 free-range egg, whisked, extra, for brushing
Dutch cocoa powder, for dusting
Crème anglaise (page 230), to serve

Caramel and hazelnut filling
190 g (6 3/4 oz) hazelnuts
125 g (4 1/2 oz) dark muscovado sugar
100 ml (3 1/2 fl oz) thickened (whipping) cream
60 g (2 1/4 oz) unsalted butter, chopped

Chocolate ganache
350 ml (12 fl oz) thin (pouring) cream
400 g (14 oz) bitter dark couverture chocolate, chopped

Put the flour, butter and caster sugar in a food processor and process until the mixture resembles fine breadcrumbs. Combine the vanilla extract with the lightly whisked egg, add to the food processor and process until the mixture just comes together. Form the mixture into a ball, then wrap in plastic and refrigerate for 1 hour.

Butter and flour a 26 cm (10 1/2 inch) loose-based fluted tart tin. Lightly flour your work surface and rolling pin, then roll out the pastry to a round big enough to line the tin, about 3 mm (1/8 inch) thick. Roll the pastry around the rolling pin and then gently unroll it over the tin, easing it into the side as you go. Trim the edge and refrigerate for another 30 minutes.

Meanwhile, preheat the oven to 180°C (350°F). Line the pastry with a sheet of baking paper and pie weights or uncooked rice. Blind bake for 10 minutes, then remove the paper and weights, prick the base a few times and brush the base and side with the extra egg to seal. Bake for another 10 minutes or until golden. Set aside to cool completely, but leave the oven on.

To make the caramel and hazelnut filling, spread the hazelnuts on a baking tray lined with baking paper and roast for about 8 minutes or until golden. Tip onto a clean tea towel and rub with the towel to remove the papery skins. Coarsely chop the hazelnuts.

Put the muscovado sugar, cream and butter in a heavy-based saucepan and bring to the boil over medium heat. Reduce the heat and simmer, stirring occasionally, for 8 minutes, then remove from the heat and stir in the hazelnuts. Leave to cool to room temperature.

To make the chocolate ganache, pour the cream into a saucepan and gently bring to a simmer. Remove from the heat and add the chocolate. Allow to stand for about 5 minutes to allow the chocolate to melt, then mix with a spatula until smooth. Leave to cool to room temperature.

To assemble, spread the caramel and hazelnut filling over the base of the tart case, then spread the chocolate ganache over the top and smooth with a spatula. Refrigerate for 3 hours or until set.

When you are ready to serve, generously dust the tart with cocoa powder, cut into wedges and serve with the crème anglaise alongside.

Coconut sago with passionfruit mousse

Serves 4

The classic combo of coconut and sago is so good – you don't even need to add the passionfruit mousse. I just love it spooned over fruit salad, which makes a very simple dessert.

375 g (13 oz) sago, rinsed well
60 ml (2 fl oz/¼ cup) coconut cream
(Kara brand is the best)
pinch of sea salt
2 passionfruit, to serve

Passionfruit mousse
125 ml (4 fl oz/½ cup) milk
4 free-range egg yolks
75 g (2½ oz/⅓ cup) caster
(superfine) sugar
100 ml (3½ fl oz) strained fresh
passionfruit pulp, at room temperature
1 titanium-strength gelatine sheet
80 ml (2½ fl oz/⅓ cup) thick
(double) cream
80 ml (2½ fl oz/⅓ cup) thin
(pouring) cream

To make the passionfruit mousse, gently warm the milk in a saucepan. Whisk the egg yolks and sugar in a bowl until pale and creamy, then incorporate the passionfruit pulp. Gradually pour the warm milk over the top, whisking to combine, then pour back into the saucepan. Cook over low heat, stirring constantly, for about 10 minutes or until the mixture thickens enough to coat the back of a spoon.

Soak the gelatine sheet in a little cold water until soft, then gently squeeze out the excess water. Add the gelatine to the passionfruit mixture and stir until dissolved. Pass the mixture through a fine sieve into a bowl set over iced water and stir until cool.

When the mixture is almost set (this could take up to 1 hour), whisk the thick and thin cream together in a separate bowl to form soft peaks. Gently fold the cream through the passionfruit mixture. Divide the mixture among four glasses and refrigerate for about 30 minutes or until set.

Meanwhile, bring a large saucepan of water to the boil. Add the sago and bring to a simmer. Cook, whisking frequently, for 12–15 minutes. Watch the granules and drain immediately once they reach the point just before they become transparent. If they are left too long they will dissolve into a sticky, gluey mess. Rinse the sago under cold running water to stop any further cooking and cool down; by this stage the sago should be transparent. Mix the sago with the coconut cream and sea salt.

Spoon the sago on top of the passionfruit mousse and serve garnished with the fresh passionfruit pulp.

Note
You will need about 6 fresh passionfruit to yield 100 ml (3½ fl oz) strained pulp. It's important that the pulp is at room temperature when you add it to the egg yolks and sugar, otherwise the mixture may curdle when you add the warm milk.

COCONUT SAGO WITH PASSIONFRUIT MOUSSE

240

Raspberry coconut pudding

Serves 8–10

I love this pudding because you can serve it straight from the oven – choose a gorgeous old-school pie dish that can go to the table, and there's no fiddling around with pastry or turning things out. It's the perfect dinner party dessert because it's fail-proof!

110 g (3 3/4 oz) raspberry jam
250 g (9 oz / 1 2/3 cups) plain
    (all-purpose) flour
3 teaspoons baking powder
350 g (12 oz) caster (superfine) sugar
100 g (3 1/2 oz) desiccated coconut
3 free-range eggs, lightly beaten
350 ml (12 fl oz) milk
1 teaspoon natural vanilla extract
150 g (5 1/2 oz) unsalted butter, melted
icing (confectioners') sugar, for dusting
lightly whipped cream, to serve

Preheat the oven to 180°C (350°F).

Spread the jam over the base of a 2 litre (70 fl oz/8 cup) pie dish. Sift the flour and baking powder into a bowl, then add the sugar, coconut, eggs, milk, vanilla and melted butter and whisk until just combined.

Pour the pudding batter into the pie dish over the jam and bake for 40–50 minutes or until the top is golden brown and the centre has a light spring when pressed with your finger.

Remove the pudding from the oven and allow to cool slightly before dusting with icing sugar and taking to the table. Serve with a dollop of whipped cream.

241

RASPBERRY COCONUT PUDDING

Oeufs à la neige

Serves 6

One of the very first desserts I ever made. This is classic French and, although simple, it is sublime. The taste and texture are so delicate.

560 ml (19 1/4 fl oz / 2 1/4 cups) milk
1 vanilla bean, split lengthways
1 strip orange zest, no white pith
2 large free-range eggs
35 g (1 1/4 oz) caster (superfine) sugar

Meringues
225 ml (7 1/2 fl oz) milk
4 large free-range egg whites
110 g (3 3/4 oz / 1/2 cup) caster (superfine) sugar
1/2 teaspoon natural vanilla extract

Pour the milk into a small saucepan. Scrape in the vanilla seeds and add the vanilla bean and orange zest. Heat the milk until almost boiling. Cover, remove from the heat and set aside for at least 30 minutes to infuse the flavours.

Return the milk to a simmer. Whisk the eggs and sugar in a bowl until smooth, then gradually add the hot milk, whisking constantly. Pour the mixture back into the pan and cook over low heat, stirring constantly with a wooden spoon, for about 10 minutes or until the mixture thickens enough to coat the back of the spoon. Don't let it boil or you will have scrambled eggs. Strain the custard into a bowl, cover and refrigerate until cold.

To make the meringues, put the milk in a deep, wide saucepan and add enough water to give a depth of about 5 cm (2 inches). Place the pan over low heat and bring to a gentle simmer.

Meanwhile, use an electric mixer with a whisk attachment to whisk the egg whites until they form soft peaks, then gradually add the sugar and vanilla extract and continue whisking until the meringue is stiff.

Using two large spoons dipped in cold water, form large egg-shaped ovals of meringue and gently drop them into the simmering liquid as you go. Do this in a couple of batches – don't overcrowd the pan and don't let the meringues touch. Cook on one side for about 8 minutes, then turn and cook on the other side for about 4 minutes. Remove and drain the meringues on paper towel.

Pour the custard into bowls and top with the meringues to serve.

OEUFS À LA NEIGE

Plum cobbler

Serves 4–6

Another old-school dessert; there is a reason why this is such a classic and that is because it just tastes so good. Most stone fruit work really well with this recipe.

60 g (2 1/4 oz) chilled butter, chopped, plus extra for greasing
800 g (1 lb 12 oz) plums, peeled and roughly chopped
110 g (3 3/4 oz / 3/4 cup) self-raising flour
55 g (2 oz / 1/4 cup) caster (superfine) sugar
1 teaspoon ground cinnamon
1 free-range egg yolk
60 ml (2 fl oz / 1/4 cup) buttermilk
40 g (1 1/2 oz / 1/4 cup) roasted hazelnuts, roughly chopped
40 g (1 1/2 oz / 1/4 cup) blanched roasted almonds, roughly chopped
ice cream or whipped cream, to serve

Preheat the oven to 180°C (350°F). Grease a deep pie dish with butter and add the plums.

Sift the flour, sugar and cinnamon into a bowl and rub in the butter with your fingers. Stir in the egg yolk and enough of the buttermilk to make a sticky dough, then drop heaped teaspoons of the mixture over the plums and sprinkle with the combined hazelnuts and almonds.

Bake the cobbler for about 40 minutes or until golden brown. Remove from the oven and allow to rest for at least 10 minutes.

Serve the cobbler with ice cream or whipped cream.

Chocolate mousse with hazelnut praline

Serves 4

You could set this mousse in a larger bowl, then scoop it out onto plates if you like – this might be a bit more festive if you are doubling the recipe to serve a larger group.

Pour the cream into a saucepan and gently bring to a simmer. Remove from the heat, add the chopped chocolate and stand for around 6 minutes to allow the chocolate to melt, then mix with a spatula until smooth. Whisk the coffee and egg yolks into the chocolate mixture until well combined.

Use an electric beater with a whisk attachment to whisk the egg whites until stiff peaks form. Using a large metal spoon, gently fold the egg whites into the chocolate mixture in three batches. Spoon the mixture into four glasses, cover and refrigerate for 6 hours or until set.

Meanwhile, to make the hazelnut praline, preheat the oven to 180°C (350°F). Spread the hazelnuts on a baking tray lined with baking paper and roast for about 8 minutes or until golden. Tip onto a clean tea towel and rub with the towel to remove the papery skins. Line the baking tray with a fresh sheet of paper, then place the hazelnuts back on the tray.

Combine the sugar with 60 ml (2 fl oz / $1/4$ cup) water in a small saucepan and place over low heat. When the sugar has melted, increase the heat to high and simmer until the mixture turns a deep golden colour. Watch the caramel at all times as it can burn easily. Remove from the heat and allow the bubbles to subside, then pour the caramel over the hazelnuts and leave until hard.

Break the praline into small pieces and scatter it over the chocolate mousse just before serving.

300 ml (10$1/2$ fl oz) thick (double) cream
250 g (9 oz) dark chocolate (70% cocoa solids), chopped
1$1/2$ tablespoons fresh espresso coffee
3 large free-range eggs, separated

Hazelnut praline
75 g (2$1/2$ oz / $1/2$ cup) hazelnuts
110 g (3$3/4$ oz / $1/2$ cup) caster (superfine) sugar

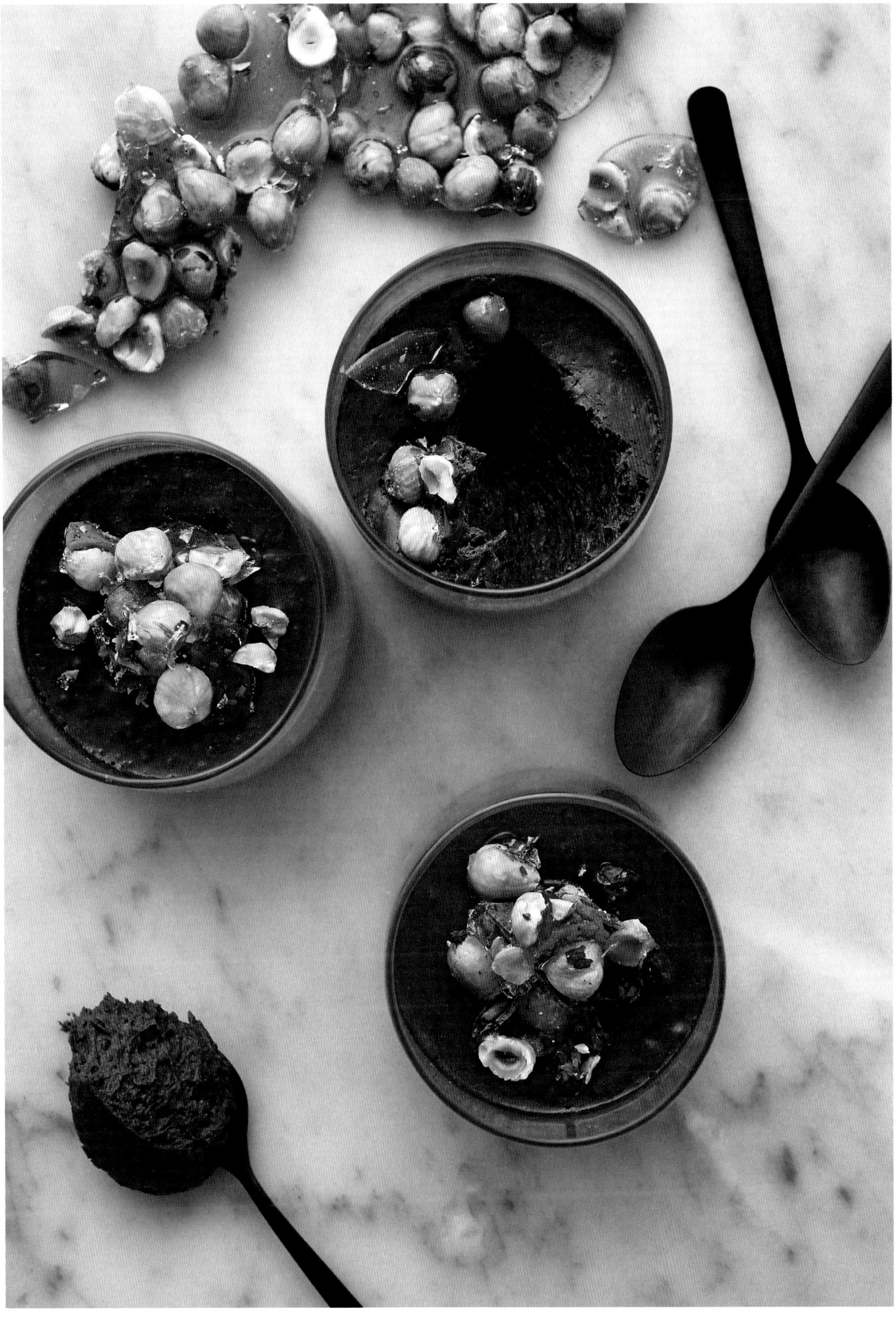

Italian apple cake

Serves 8

Take time to arrange the apples neatly so the cake looks amazing when it's cooked. If you'd prefer not to use the liqueur, it can be left out altogether and the result will still be delicious.

150 g (5$^1/_2$ oz) unsalted butter, softened
200 g (7 oz) caster (superfine) sugar
1 teaspoon natural vanilla extract
finely grated zest of 1 orange
4 free-range eggs
200 g (7 oz/1$^1/_3$ cups) plain
    (all-purpose) flour
1 teaspoon baking powder
pinch of sea salt
60 ml (2 fl oz/$^1/_4$ cup) milk
1 tablespoon orange liqueur
3 red apples
3 teaspoons lemon juice
pinch of ground cinnamon, plus extra
    for dusting
icing (confectioners') sugar, for dusting

Mascarpone cream
180 g (6 oz) mascarpone cheese
2 tablespoons thick (double) cream
3 teaspoons caster (superfine) sugar
2 teaspoons orange liqueur

Preheat the oven to 180°C (350°F). Lightly grease a 22 cm (8$^1/_2$ inch) round spring-form cake tin and line the base and side with two layers of baking paper, extending 2 cm ($^3/_4$ inch) above the side of the tin.

Use an electric mixer to beat the butter with 150 g (5$^1/_2$ oz/$^2/_3$ cup) of the caster sugar, the vanilla extract and orange zest until light and creamy. Add the eggs one at a time, beating well after each addition.

In a separate bowl, sift the flour, baking powder and sea salt. Add half the flour mixture to the butter mixture and mix until just combined, then add the milk, liqueur and remaining flour mixture and mix until the batter is smooth. Spoon the batter into the prepared tin.

Peel, core and thinly slice the apples and toss them with the lemon juice to prevent browning. Combine the remaining caster sugar with the cinnamon and toss with the apples. Arrange the apple slices in overlapping circles to cover the top of the cake.

Bake the cake for 60–65 minutes or until cooked when tested with a skewer. Stand in the tin for 10 minutes before releasing the side of the tin and leaving the cake to cool in the tin on a wire rack.

To make the mascarpone cream, beat the mascarpone, cream, sugar and liqueur with a wooden spoon until combined. Do not overmix or it may curdle.

Serve the cake warm or at room temperature with the mascarpone cream alongside. If serving at room temperature, dust the top of the cake with icing sugar and then cinnamon.

Acknowledgements

A great team of people have put this book together.

Firstly, thanks to Kate Barker, who works brilliantly on my *Good Weekend* columns with me – both you and Jess Sly did a great job during the production and editing phase.

Then Graeme, Zac and Angel, for cooking all the gorgeous food, and Clare for the desserts. As the executive chefs at Spice Temple, Rockpool Bar & Grill and Rosetta respectively you have very busy lives, but you fitted in this extra task and the food looks amazing.

The whole team at Murdoch; a massive thanks to Sue Hines, Virginia Birch, Justine Harding and Vivien Valk. These books don't make themselves and you have all put in a bit of yourselves.

Another massive thanks to my amazing business partner, Trish Richards, for being there in the trenches with me every day. It's one of the core reasons the Rockpool Group is so successful.

Once again, a huge thanks to Earl Carter – he is not only one of the greatest photographers of all time, but is surely the best human ever.

Deborah Kaloper – thank you for the clean and simple styling that makes me want to eat the food right off the plates.

Ella, thanks for slotting in to my personal team so easily and juggling my diary. Getting me to start – and, importantly, to finish – all the projects I have on is no mean feat.

Last, to my amazing family, Sam, Josephine, Macy and Indy – you all put up with me working all the time, but you understand how important quality is and that there are no short cuts.

Index

Published in 2016 by Murdoch Books, an imprint of Allen & Unwin

Murdoch Books Australia
83 Alexander Street
Crows Nest NSW 2065
Phone: +61 (0) 2 8425 0100
Fax: +61 (0) 2 9906 2218
murdochbooks.com.au
info@murdochbooks.com.au

Murdoch Books UK
Ormond House
26–27 Boswell Street
London WC1N 3JZ
Phone: +44 (0) 20 8785 5995
murdochbooks.co.uk
info@murdochbooks.co.uk

For Corporate Orders & Custom Publishing, contact our Business
Development Team at salesenquiries@murdochbooks.com.au.

Publisher: Sue Hines
Design: Vivien Valk
Editorial Manager: Virginia Birch
Editor: Justine Harding
Photographer: Earl Carter
Stylist: Deborah Kaloper
Food Production: Graeme Hunt, Zac Nicholson,
   Angel Fernandez, Clare Armstrong
Production Manager: Alexandra Gonzalez

A cataloguing-in-publication entry is available from the catalogue
of the National Library of Australia at nla.gov.au.

ISBN 978 1 74336 891 6 Australia
ISBN 978 1 74336 892 3 UK

A catalogue record for this book is available from the British Library.

Colour reproduction by Splitting Image Colour Studio Pty Ltd,
   Clayton, Victoria
Printed by 1010 Printing International Limited, China

IMPORTANT: Those who might be
at risk from the effects of salmonella
poisoning (the elderly, pregnant women,
young children and those suffering from
immune deficiency diseases) should
consult their doctor with any concerns
about eating raw eggs.

OVEN GUIDE: You may find cooking
times vary depending on the oven you
are using. For fan-forced ovens, as a
general rule, set the oven temperature
to 20°C (35°F) lower than indicated in
the recipe.

MEASURES GUIDE: We have used
20 ml (4 teaspoon) tablespoon
measures. If you are using a 15 ml
(3 teaspoon) tablespoon add an extra
teaspoon of the ingredient for each
tablespoon specified.